Learning

TO

Breathe

HOW TO CULTIVATE A
LIFE-CHANGING RELATIONSHIP
WITH THE HOLY SPIRIT

MATT MORTON

ISBN Paperback 979-8-9858080-0-1
eBook 979-8-9858080-1-8

Book Cover and Text Design by Harrington Interactive Media
Published by River and Sea Publishing, 2611 Chillingham Ct, College Station, TX 77845

Printed in the United States of America

Dedicated to the memory of my father, Glenn
R. Morton, who taught me how to think and
showed me how to persevere in my faith.

Table of Contents

CHAPTER 1

Short of Breath

---

*This is what the Sovereign LORD says
to these bones: I will make breath enter
you, and you will come to life.*

— EZEKIEL 37:5 (NASB)

One of my most humiliating moments occurred around 1989, when I was in the 8th grade. It was a Wednesday night, and my dad dropped me off for our church's youth group meeting. Like I always did, I'd spent a considerable amount of time thinking about what I was wearing and whether my hair looked cool enough to impress the girls. Not exactly spiritual thoughts, I know, but I was only thirteen years old. Overall, I was feeling pretty good about the evening. Even though I was always self-conscious at that age, my church youth group typically felt safer than the cruel hallways of my junior high school.

As I entered the church gym, I straightened my posture and lifted my head, trying to look as confident as possible. When I opened the glass doors and walked inside, I saw some of my friends and youth leaders talking, laughing, and throwing balls back and forth. Everybody was having a fun time before getting down to the more serious business of Bible study.

As soon as I walked in the door, I heard somebody shout, "Matt! Think quick!" I looked up just in time to see a perfectly thrown football speeding in my direction. One of my youth leaders threw me the ball as a way of saying hello. He wanted me to know that he saw me and was including me in their game.

It was a wonderful gesture, except that I wasn't prepared to catch the ball. With stunning speed and precision, the pointed end of that football hit me square in the solar plexus, roughly halfway between my chest and my belly button. I honestly don't remember the next several seconds. The next thing I do remember is lying flat on my back and looking at the gym ceiling far overhead. I heard what sounded like distant voices, "Matt, are you okay?" My youth leader, that young Tom Brady impersonator who had zinged the football at me, was looking down at me with concern. I couldn't help but notice that several of the girls I was hoping to impress were also looking down at me, but not with admiration on their faces. It was pity I saw in their eyes.

Oh, and I also wasn't okay. I couldn't breathe. That football had completely knocked the wind out of me. I'd heard people talk about having the wind knocked out of them before, but I didn't really understand what that meant until that moment. What's the big deal about not being able to breathe for a minute or two?

Not being able to breath for any length of time is a very big deal, as it turns out. It's terrifying, painful, and potentially dangerous. If you've never experienced it, imagine trying to draw a breath, but your lungs simply won't expand. It's like having a 100-pound rock sitting right on top of your lungs. When you try to draw air, you gasp instead, making a terrible screeching sound. You instinctively thrash your limbs, which only makes things worse. "Stay calm," my youth leader was saying. "It will be alright." But it's impossible to stay calm when you can't breathe. Your body sends loud emergency signals to your brain, and everything inside of you screams, "YOU'RE GOING TO DIE NOW!"

Thankfully, though, I didn't die that day. My lungs slowly began to expand again, as I fought hard to inhale. I was able to take deeper and deeper breaths, and after about sixty seconds everything was back to normal. But in that terrifying minute or so, I learned by experience something that I'd only known in theory: We can't function without air. If you can't breathe, you will eventually pass out. And if you go too long without air, of course, you will die.

As you might suspect, that story has a spiritual point: Trying to live the Christian life without a close relationship with the Holy Spirit is like trying to function without air in your lungs. It's just not a good idea. Many Christians are doing just that, attempting to follow Jesus without sufficient spiritual air. I believe we face a widespread spiritual crisis that is disrupting our connection to God and preventing us from becoming the people He is calling us to be. Our lives aren't working as God intended, because we are not connected to the life-giving breath of His Holy Spirit.

Jesus promised His followers lives full of spiritual power and eternal significance, but we don't often experience His power like we should. God's Word is meant to change our lives, but instead we're spiritually stagnant. We know we should tell people about Jesus, but our fear keeps us from trying. And when we do share the gospel, people often won't listen. Arguments about politics and social issues have torn our churches into factions, and we can't seem to mend them. Pastors, Christian leaders, and everyday believers are falling into sin at an alarming rate, leaving destruction and disillusionment in their wake. The Christian life should be full of power and joy, but it feels like drudgery and rote religion instead. We find ourselves gasping for breath, wondering how things have gone so wrong.

But there is good news: The Holy Spirit has the power to raise the dead and wake up those who sleep. And if you know Jesus Christ, His Spirit already lives inside of you. Jesus wasn't lying when He promised His disciples lives of purity and purpose. God wants to warm up our cold hearts and breathe His air into our lungs. The Holy Spirit who raised Jesus from the dead wants to give us greater lives than we can even imagine (Romans 8:11).

We Need a Reformation

If you feel like something is missing in your spiritual life, you are not alone. When I was a seminary student, I remember one of my professors saying, "The American church doesn't need another short-lived revival. We need another Reformation." His point was that we have drifted so far from the life God wants for us that we need to rethink almost everything about how we approach our spiritual lives: our theology, our habits, our worship services, and so much more. Much like the Protestant Reformation of the 16th Century, we need to take a hard look at where things have gone wrong and how things need to change.

Recent research also supports the idea that our Christian lives aren't working as God intended. Ronald Sider's book *The Scandal of the Evangelical Conscience*, cites troubling statistics demonstrating that the lives of Christians often don't look much different from anybody else's. Rates of divorce, sexual immorality, racism, and marital abuse are as high among Christians as they are among other groups, and maybe even higher.[1] How can that be? After all, we go to church, listen to sermons, sing Christian songs, and read Christian books. We *want* to know and obey God, and we're constantly learning information about God, but for some reason He doesn't seem to make a big difference in our lives. How can we know so much about Jesus, and even teach other people about Him, and yet fall so grievously short in our own spiritual lives?

Partly because of these failures, young people are increasingly skeptical about Christianity. In a 2020 study of more than 1,500 young adults from Christian families, the Barna group found that only 10% of them could be described as "resilient disciples." Resilient disciples are Christians who have deep and meaningful connections, not only with their churches, but also with Jesus. Resilient disciples say that Jesus has changed their lives in profound ways. They regularly experience His presence and His power. On the plus side, it's encouraging that there are still at least *some* resilient disciples of Jesus among younger generations. What is tragic, though, is that 90% of the young adults in this survey came from Christian homes, yet they don't feel like their faith makes much of a difference in their lives. Nearly a quarter of them have left the faith altogether.[2] These young men and women grew up in church, they were exposed to Christian teaching, and they had Christian parents. They sang all the worship songs, heard all the sermons, and went to youth group. While it's true that young people from faithful Christian homes sometimes go astray, these statistics suggest that there is a bigger problem at hand. We seem to be missing something in our quest to raise up the next generation of Christians.

What if younger generations are not captivated by Christianity, because older Christians aren't showing them anything particularly captivating? Maybe too few of us, no matter our age, are captivated by Jesus. All too often we simply go through the motions and participate in Christian rituals without the power and joy that Jesus promised to His disciples.

Consider your own spiritual life for a moment. Would you say that you really know God well, or do you often feel distant from Him? Do you regularly experience a deep and abiding connection with Him? Are you becoming more and more like Jesus as the years go by? Or have you struggled with the same old sins for years on end with no real improvement? Does your life bring honor and praise to Jesus, or is your walk with Him sort of ho-hum? If we're honest with ourselves, most of us know that our spiritual lives aren't really where God wants them to be. We believe that Jesus *can* change lives, but He hasn't really changed *our* lives. Where have we gone wrong? What in the world are we missing?

I believe what we're missing is a life-giving connection to the Holy Spirit. We are short of spiritual breath because we aren't walking with God's Spirit. Until we recover that vital connection, we will find ourselves spiritually weak and lifeless. We won't know God as deeply as we desire, and we won't have the eternal impact we hope to have on those around us.

Throughout this book, I'll use the analogy of air to describe the Holy Spirit. It's a biblical analogy. The Bible often compares the Holy Spirit to air, wind, or breath. In fact, the very words that the Bible uses for "spirit" can be translated "wind," or "breath." It's no exaggeration to say that the Holy Spirit is as important to our spiritual lives as air is to our physical lives. Even for Christians, it is possible to live a sort of spiritual half-life. We can be technically alive, but still struggling, confused, and joyless. That's the state of many Christians at this very moment. We have trusted in Jesus for eternal life, but we aren't walking with Him through the Spirit's power. We are alive in Christ, but desperately short of spiritual breath. And when we're short of breath, our lives won't work as He intended.

Bad Spiritual Air

Let me give you one example from my own life to illustrate what I'm talking about. Many years ago, my wife and I took our three kids out to dinner one evening. At the time, our kids were quite young – all of them under 8 years old or so – and the restaurant was the type of place where you have to put your name on a list and wait until a table is available. Anybody who has young children knows that this situation is a recipe for trouble if the wait gets too long. When you have three young and restless kids in tow, your goal is to sit down, eat, and leave the restaurant as quickly as possible. Otherwise, they'll get tired and cranky, and they might cause a scene.

On this particular evening, though, the hostess assured us that the wait for a table would only be around 20-25 minutes. Since it was still early in the evening, we figured we could manage that. However, it actually took much longer before our table was ready. Much, much longer. After 30 minutes had passed, I politely inquired again when we might sit down. "Very soon," said the hostess. "Not long now." But it wasn't true. After 45 minutes, I asked again, with a bit less patience this time. I wasn't really rude, but I allowed just enough frustration into my voice to let her know I meant business. After an hour of waiting, I complained again, even less patiently this time. We debated whether we should leave the restaurant altogether, but by now we were stuck; we didn't really have any other good options. Finally, after about an hour and fifteen minutes, something snapped inside of me. No, I didn't hit anybody or get myself arrested. But I dramatically jumped up from the bench where we had been waiting and went around behind the hostess' stand. I grabbed her waiting list and began to question her in a frustrated voice about why certain other people had been seated ahead of us. I explained to her in no uncertain terms that we had been treated in an unacceptable manner and this would certainly be our final visit to this restaurant and we would tell all of our friends to avoid it like the plague. I spoke eloquently and at length about this grievous miscarriage of justice and why we deserved restitution. She found a way to seat us pretty quickly after that, but I felt ashamed of myself. (For the record, we did visit again eventually, and I didn't publicly malign the place later).

Now, I'm not proud of that moment at all. Whenever I remember it, I cringe. You might be cringing also. On the other hand, you might be thinking I did the right and reasonable thing! After all, I waited for nearly an hour before I lost my ever-loving mind. And I had hungry kids with me! There were all sorts of good reasons for me to lose my temper in that moment. But I know I was in the wrong, of course. It's never acceptable to grab the list from the hostess's hand and insist that she seat you right away, even if you think you have good reasons to do so. My actions sprang from pride and a sense of entitlement, no matter how justified I felt in the moment. If we're honest, we almost *always* feel that we have good reasons for our sin. We rarely sin in the absence of provocation or pressure. The pressure merely shows what's already inside of us.

My circumstances didn't *make* me lose my temper; they simply revealed that I have a heart prone to anger.

It wasn't the first time I learned the hard way that, under the wrong circumstances, my sinful and selfish desires can break through my carefully cultivated façade of righteousness. My behavior that evening was nothing less than sinful: impatience and uncontrolled anger over something that wasn't really all that important. In the heat of the moment, all I could think about was myself; I ignored the feelings of the hostess, the embarrassment of my family, and even my own commitment to reflect the patience and grace of Jesus.

Where did my outburst come from? It came from what the Bible calls my flesh, from my desire to have my own way at all costs. The pressure I was under revealed the state of my heart. At that moment, I wasn't breathing the right air. Instead of being filled by the Holy Spirit, I was full of myself. I was breathing bad spiritual air. Consequently, I exhaled what was inside my heart, and it wasn't pretty at all.

You probably have similar stories of spiritual failure. Maybe you have some stories that are even worse. To be honest, I haven't told you about my very worst moments. If I did, you'd probably stop reading this book. All of us feel ashamed sometimes at the gap between who we are right now and who we know God wants us to be. The good news is that there is always hope. It's never too late to learn how to breathe.

"I don't want my life to be explainable without the Holy Spirit."
— FRANCIS CHAN[3]

There is Always Hope

I love to read biographies of great men and women of the Christian faith. I'm inspired by men like George Mueller, an evangelist and missionary who opened several orphanages in England in the 19th century. His orphanages saved more than 10,000 children from poverty during his lifetime, and hundreds of thousands more after his death. Mueller's work was made possible through his deep and rich prayer life. He constantly asked for God's provision, walking daily in the power of the Holy Spirit. His ministry was miraculously effective because he was filled with God's Spirit.

I'm stirred by stories of women like Corrie ten Boom, the daughter of a Dutch watchmaker who was arrested during World War II for sheltering Jews in her home. Corrie and her family saved hundreds of people from certain death at the hands of the Nazis. While she was imprisoned in the horrific Ravensbruck concentration camp, Corrie still read her Bible every day, clinging desperately to God's promises. She risked her life to share the gospel, and she started a Bible study for her fellow prisoners. She even learned to forgive the cruel guards who mistreated her, and who were responsible for the death of her beloved sister. After the war, she traveled all over the world, preaching the good news that God's forgiveness can save even the hardest hearts. The Word of God had so completely transformed her heart that she constantly exhaled the good news of the gospel.

There are literally hundreds of examples like this to choose from, stories of Spirit-filled people who changed the world for Jesus. There are pioneering missionaries like Hudson Taylor, Adoniram Judson, and Elisabeth Elliot, who constantly relied on God's Spirit and saw Him move through their lives in powerful ways. Or preachers like Jonathan Edwards and Billy Graham, who led great movements of God, through which tens of thousands of people came to know Jesus. These stories remind me that when God's people are connected to His Spirit, truly great things can happen.

And it's not only famous Christians who inspire me. It's also ordinary Christians who serve God faithfully, even though few people know their names. I think of my friend Bill, whose prayer life is so rich that you can see the love of Jesus written on his face. I remember a woman I once knew named Vi, who could recite entire books of the New Testament from memory, and whose eyes constantly reflected the joy of her Savior. These are ordinary Christians who learned how to breathe Spirit-filled air.

I want to be more like these heroes of the faith, full of the Christ-like character and power that the Holy Spirit can provide. You're probably reading this book because you want that sort of life also. You long to reflect the love and the power of Jesus on a consistent basis. You deeply desire to have an impact on other people's lives that will last for eternity. Do you believe that kind of life is actually possible for ordinary followers of Jesus? I believe that it is, when we cultivate a life-giving relationship with the Holy Spirit.

God's Word says that He wants to transform everything about us from the inside out: our thoughts, our words, our habits, and our relationships (2 Cor 3:18; Rom 8:29). He wants to use us in powerful ways to change other people's lives. His Spirit has the power to accomplish things that we can't even imagine.

The process of spiritual transformation will be slow and painful, though. We will have to reexamine attitudes and behaviors that have defined our lives for as long as we can remember. We will have to take a long, hard look at our priorities. God will ask us to let go of some things we hold dear, and to care deeply about things we've never considered. He will ask us to get rid of some old habits and develop new ones. None of this will happen overnight. It will take a lifetime.

To begin this journey of learning to breathe spiritual air, we have to honestly ask ourselves, "Do my thoughts, my feelings, my priorities, and my actions increasingly reflect the character of Jesus? If not, where am I falling short?" When we ask those questions honestly, we will see how far we still have to go on the path of spiritual transformation. Once we understand where we are, we can begin to move forward. It will take humility and bravery to admit that we aren't where we should be, but this terrifying honesty is critical if the Spirit is going to do His transformative work in our lives. Wherever you find yourself on the pathway to spiritual maturity, God is calling you to simply take the next step. My hope is that this book will provide you with the tools you need to move forward in your spiritual journey as you seek to develop a closer walk with the Holy Spirit.

Since we live by the Spirit, let us
keep in step with the Spirit.
— GALATIANS 5:25

One Breath at a Time

Not long ago, I read an article about a man named Joe Newman, who lives in Sarasota, Florida. Joe is 107 years old; he's lived through two world wars, the Great Depression, the Cold War, and now he's even lived through two major pandemics. He drives around town in a bright red Mercedes convertible with his young fiancé Anita (she's a spring chicken at merely 100 years old). When asked what it means to be 107 years old, Joe said, "[It] means you keep breathing day after day."[4] I like that answer; it's short but profound. Joe isn't thinking about how things will be when he's 108 or 109. He's taking it one day at a time, because he realizes that today might be the only day he has left. In fact, he's taking things one *breath* at a time.

Every long journey begins with one step, and every life is lived one day at a time. As we move forward in our discussion of the Holy Spirit, it's not a bad idea to live like Joe Newman. We will not reach spiritual maturity overnight. Instead of becoming anxious or depressed at the gap between where we are and where we ought to be, let's take things one breath at a time. Day in and day out, week after week, month after month, and year after year, we want to build habits and attitudes that will slowly and steadily draw us closer to Jesus and help us to know God in deeper ways. We build those attitudes and habits by consistently putting ourselves in a position where we can hear and obey the voice of the Holy Spirit. We want to breathe in the air of God's Spirit, to live by the spiritual oxygen that He provides us.

This book is designed to help us learn how to breathe the Spirit's air. We'll examine what sort of people we'll be when we start to walk with the Holy Spirit. We'll talk about how to develop habits that will allow us to respond to the Spirit's voice. Before we do that, though, let's spend some time getting acquainted with the Holy Spirit Himself. Who is He and what exactly does He do?

CHAPTER 2

Who is the Holy Spirit?

*"Undoubtedly the least understood person
of the Godhead is the Holy Spirit."*

— CHARLES RYRIE[5]

I have a confession to make: I never fully outgrew my childhood fascination with construction sites. I can watch bulldozers, backhoes, excavators, cranes, and concrete trucks for hours as they go about their business. Sometimes I imagine what it would be like to drive one of those big machines myself; it's an opportunity I've never had but one that I've often dreamed about. Not long ago, our church finished construction on a new building, and I loved watching the building process. Sometimes I would take my 10-year-old son to the construction site with me, just so it wouldn't seem weird that a 40-something pastor was eagerly staring at the giant machines as they broke up the ground, moved dirt around, and hoisted steel beams into the air. I secretly hoped that the contractor might notice me and invite me to drive his bulldozer for a few minutes. Sadly, that never happened, probably because he figured (correctly) that I would hurt myself or somebody else.

As much as I enjoy watching large construction vehicles, I also enjoy seeing how smaller machines play their part. Hand-held equipment like power drills, saws, and jackhammers fascinate me. One of my favorite machines is the breaker hammer, which crushes concrete and rocks to make way for new construction on the ground. Talk about a power tool!

Recently, I began wondering where all the awesome power in those tools comes from. I have a few power tools at home, but nothing approaches the sheer force displayed by these construction tools. After a quick Google search, I learned that the powerful tools used for major construction projects are often pneumatic, meaning that they're powered by air. The machines are connected to strong air compressors, which force air through a hose, delivering an immense amount of power for the job at hand. Compressed air packs a punch, as anyone who has seen these tools in action can tell you. Air is much more powerful than we often realize. Air can produce enough force to smash concrete.

"The Holy Spirit is a person, not a vague force. Thus, He is someone with whom we can have a personal relationship."
— MILLARD ERICKSON[6]

The Air of the Spirit

The Scripture frequently uses the imagery of powerful air, or wind, to describe the Holy Spirit. In fact, the word "pneumatic" comes from the Greek word "pneuma," which means "wind," or "breath." Whenever you see the word "spirit" in the New Testament, it's a translation of that Greek word. That includes references to the Holy Spirit, the third member of the Trinity. Much like the wind that powers those pneumatic tools, the Holy Spirit is powerful, yet invisible. And much like the air that fills our lungs, we would die without Him. But it is important for us to understand that the Holy Spirit is different from the wind in one critical respect. The wind isn't alive, but the Holy Spirit is very much alive. In fact, He is the Source of life itself, the living and personal breath of God.

Not long ago, Lifeway Research surveyed American evangelicals about their theological beliefs. They were surprised to find that most evangelical Christians (59%) don't think of the Holy Spirit as being alive. Instead, they described the Holy Spirit as an impersonal force, almost like a blob of spiritual goo.[7] Apparently, most Christians don't think of the Spirit as a living, conscious Person. They understand the Holy Spirit to be more like the Force in the classic Star Wars movies. If you have seen the movies, you remember Luke Skywalker's tiny green mentor, Yoda. He describes the mysterious Force like this: "For my ally is the force, and a powerful ally it is. Life creates it, makes it grow. Its energy surrounds us and binds us. You must feel the Force around you; here, between you, me, the tree, the rock, everywhere, yes." (Despite being extremely wise, Yoda seems to have failed grammar class). The Force, he tells Luke, is a powerful and omnipresent spiritual entity, but it is not really alive. Instead, the Force is generated by the life that *already* exists in the Universe. Many Christians think the Holy Spirit is basically the same way, but that is not how the Bible describes Him. As long as our beliefs about the Holy Spirit are drawn from pop culture, from other world religions, or from our own imaginations, we are going to have inaccurate perceptions of who He is.

Because we don't have accurate beliefs about the Holy Spirit, we often struggle to know Him and to walk with Him. And as long as we struggle to walk with the Spirit, our Christian lives will fall short of what God desires for us. Remember, the main goal of this book is to offer some practical tools to help us lead Spirit-filled lives. A Spirit-filled life is one in which we carefully listen to the Holy Spirit's voice on a daily basis as He makes us more and more like Jesus. This sort of spiritual transformation happens over time, as we learn to obey God's voice rather than our own sinful desires. As we develop a closer relationship with the Holy Spirit, we'll come to know God in deeper ways, and we will increasingly reflect His perfect character. In order to cultivate that type of connection with the Spirit, though, we need to first understand a little bit about who He is.

We are going to begin our journey with the Holy Spirit, then, by learning more about Him. Who is He? What does He do? Why does He matter? We will try to answer those questions concisely in this chapter. This will be the most theologically intense chapter in the book, so please bear with me. This will take some concentration, but understanding what the Bible says about the Holy Spirit is worth the effort.

"When we consider the earth without form and void, methinks it is like the valley full of dead and dry bones. Can these live? Can this confused mass of matter be formed into a beautiful world? Yes, if a spirit of life from God enter into it."[8]
— MATTHEW HENRY

In the Beginning

If we want to understand the Holy Spirit, we need to start at the beginning, in the book of Genesis. The Old Testament doesn't have as much to say about the Holy Spirit as the New Testament does, but that doesn't mean He wasn't around or active before Jesus came. The Spirit simply became more visible to *us* after He came upon the church on the Day of Pentecost (Acts 2). But if we read the Old Testament carefully, we'll see that He has always been around, and He has always been an active participant in God's work. In fact, His participation goes all the way back to the very beginning of the world.

The Spirit makes His first appearance in Genesis 1:2, before the creation of the world. The earth was "*formless and void*" back then. No mountains, no atmosphere, no continents, no animals or trees, and no people. But the Spirit of God was there, "*hovering over the face of the waters.*" The impression that Genesis gives us is that the Holy Spirit was waiting for the Father to start talking, to give Him instructions. From Psalm 104:30 we learn that the sea, the earth, and the creatures in them were created when God sent forth His Spirit to do the work. We see it happen in those first few verses of Genesis. God the Father begins speaking. As the Father speaks, the Spirit goes forth to do what He says. "*Let there be light,*" God says, and the Holy Spirit flips the switch. From the first day until the sixth day, the Spirit of God was present and active in creating the world. That tells us that the Holy Spirit was around long before the world was made, but also that the Spirit does the work of God. Genesis 1 gives us an early peek at what the Scripture explains in more detail later: The Holy Spirit *is* God. He is not merely an impersonal force, somehow inferior to the Father or the Son, but He is fully equal to God in His nature and in His power.

Father, Son, and Holy Spirit

When we get to the New Testament, the deity (the "God-ness") of the Holy Spirit becomes even clearer to us. He is consistently named, along with the Father and the Son, as a member of the Trinity. If you're rusty on your theology, the Trinity is the distinctly Christian understanding of God's nature. Christians worship one God who exists in three Persons: Father, Son, and Holy Spirit.[9] The Three are equal in their nature, but distinct in their personalities and roles. It is a mystery, but the doctrine of the Trinity is central to our understanding of God. The Holy Spirit is every bit as much God as the Father and the Son are, and He is every bit as critical to our salvation and our spiritual life.

In Matthew 28:18–20, known as the Great Commission, Jesus commanded His disciples to *"go and make disciples of all the nations, baptizing them in the name of the Father, and of the Son, and of the Holy Spirit."* What's important to notice in this passage is that Jesus doesn't say, "the *names* of the Father, and of the Son, and of the Holy Spirit." Instead, He indicates that the Three members of the Trinity share one name, presumably the very name of God. They are distinct, yet equal. There are other places in the New Testament where we see all three members of the Trinity named together like this. For example, in 2 Corinthians 13:14, Paul says, *"The grace of the Lord Jesus Christ, and the love of God, and the fellowship of the Holy Spirit, be with you all."* In Ephesians 1, a passage too long to quote here, Paul talks about the role of each member of the Trinity in our salvation. The Father predestined us, the Son redeemed us with His blood, and the Spirit sealed us, providing us with a guarantee that God will one day save us for good. Over and over in Scripture, we see that the Spirit is a full member of the Godhead.

Not only is He repeatedly named alongside the Father and the Son, but the New Testament also attributes to the Holy Spirit characteristics that only God possesses. For example, He knows the very thoughts of God (1 Corinthians 2:9–13), which means that He is all-knowing. He is also eternal, meaning that He has always existed and He always will (Hebrews 9:14). He is capable of raising people from the dead, and in fact, He is said to have raised Jesus (Romans 8:11). The Bible leaves us no room to doubt that the Holy Spirit is every bit as knowledgeable, powerful, and ever-present as the other members of the Trinity.

"The Spirit is the executive of the Godhead. Whatever God does, He does by the Spirit."[10]
— CHARLES HODGE

The Spirit is a Person

It might seem obvious, but if the Holy Spirit is God, then He isn't an impersonal force. Instead, He is truly alive and aware, able to relate to the other members of the Trinity, as well as to you and me. That is why throughout this book, I consistently refer to the Holy Spirit as "He," rather than "it." If we return for a moment to the world of Star Wars, we can see that His personhood is the primary thing that makes the Holy Spirit different from the Force. The Force is completely impersonal; the Force doesn't have thoughts or feelings. On the other hand, the Holy

Spirit thinks and feels. He also speaks and tells people what to say and do. Far from being an undefined blob of spiritual goo, the Holy Spirit is every bit as much of a Person as the Father and the Son are. When Jesus described the Holy Spirit to His disciples, He consistently spoke about Him using what we call the third person singular masculine pronoun. If you have forgotten your 7th grade English grammar class, that's a fancy way of saying that Jesus called the Holy Spirit "Him," and not "it." In John 16:13–14 (NASB), Jesus said, *"But when He, the Spirit of truth, comes, He will guide you into all the truth; for He will not speak on His own initiative, but whatever He hears, He will speak; and He will disclose to you what is to come. He will glorify Me, for He will take of Mine and will disclose it to you."* Notice that the Spirit is not only described in personal terms, but He does things that an impersonal force could never do. He comes to people, He guides them, He speaks, and He listens.

You might be wondering why this point matters to us. After all, the purpose of this book is to help us know God and walk with the Holy Spirit, not to help us write a theological treatise about His nature. But here's why it matters that the Spirit isn't just a force: We cannot have a relationship with a blob of spiritual goo. We have relationships with *people we care about and understand,* not with forces. Think one more time about Yoda's Force. If you've seen Star Wars, you'll know that nobody talks to the Force, and the Force doesn't talk to anybody either. People manipulate the Force and use it for their own purposes, good and bad. The Force offers power, but it's character changes depending on the person using it. The evil Emperor Palpatine can use the Force just as easily as Yoda because the Force doesn't have any preferences or characteristics of its own. It isn't a person, in other words. The Holy Spirit, on the other hand, is very much a Person we can have a relationship with. Unlike the Force, the Spirit's personality stays the same whether I know Him or not. And He doesn't offer His power to just anybody for any reason whatsoever, but instead He offers His power to those who will submit to God and seek to do His will. There is no "dark side" of the Holy Spirit. To the contrary, His personality perfectly and consistently reflects the nature of God. He is always holy, always good, and He always tells the truth. Again, He is like God because He is God.

Now that we understand a little bit about the Spirit's deity and personality, let's talk about a few of the things the Spirit does. What role does He play in the world, and in our lives?

The Spirit Gives Life to the World

When my son Samuel was born, he was initially unable to breathe on his own. Since he was our third child, I had a sense of what a normal baby ought to sound like in those first moments after birth. Usually a baby is silent for a brief moment, as he leaves his mother's womb and experiences the shock of entering an entirely new world. But then the baby takes a breath and begins to cry. That cry is a sign that the child has life, that there is breath in his lungs. As much as parents eventually grow tired of hearing their babies cry, it's even worse when they *don't* cry. If a baby never cries, something is terribly wrong. When Samuel was born, the silence in that delivery room was deafening. He failed to fill his lungs with air because they were completely full of fluid. I watched with a feeling of dread and helplessness as this child we had eagerly awaited turned blue and slowly stopped moving. The nurses in the delivery room frantically worked to clear out his nose, hoping that they could create a pathway for the air to begin flowing. After a few moments, however, it was clear that he needed more help than they could provide for him in the delivery room. They whisked him away to the NICU, where he was placed on a respirator, a breathing machine designed to force air into his underdeveloped lungs. Samuel spent nearly a week on that respirator, until he was able to breath on his own. For six days, that breathing machine kept him alive; without it, our son would have perished.

Think of the Holy Spirit as the world's respirator. He gives life to everything in creation, including you and me. In Job 33:4, the writer says, "*The Spirit of God has made me; the breath of the Almighty gives me life.*" Notice the present tense verb, "gives." Job acknowledges that the Spirit made him, but he also knows that the Spirit keeps him alive on a daily basis, as well. That's not only true of Job, by the way; it's true of the entire world. If the Holy Spirit were completely removed from the world, life as we know it would cease to exist. The Spirit is God's air, the very oxygen that keeps the world and everything in it alive.

When God created Adam and Eve, it was His Breath, His Spirit, that He breathed into their nostrils in the Garden of Eden (Genesis 2:7). God's original design for humanity was for us to be both physically and spiritually alive through the power that the Holy Spirit provides. As long as Adam and Eve stayed connected to God, they were alive in every sense of the word. Moment by moment, they inhaled the air of the Garden of Eden, and they inhaled the air of the Spirit of God. Their real problems only started after they chose to disobey God by eating from the tree that He had forbidden. The consequence of their sin, as Paul tells us in the book of Romans, was death. Adam and Eve, and all of us descended from them, died spiritually on the day that they disobeyed God. They were separated from the live-giving presence of the Holy Spirit and kicked out of the Garden of Eden.

That is what death actually means, by the way: separation from God. Physical death is simply the inevitable consequence of spiritual death. Estrangement from the Holy Spirit is like removing a sick patient from a respirator. He might stay alive for a little while without it, but death is inevitable without air. The Spirit gives life, and the Spirit sustains life. Without Him, all is lost. Our bodies will remain alive temporarily, but a dead spirit always leads to a dead body. Ashes to ashes, and dust to dust.

The Spirit gives life; the flesh counts for nothing.
— JOHN 6:63

The Spirit Gives Life to God's People

The biggest problem humanity faces, then, is how to overcome the spiritual death that we inherited from Adam and Eve. In Romans 5:12 (NASB), Paul says, *"Just as through one man sin entered into the world, and death through sin . . . so death spread to all men, because all sinned."* Adam and Eve's disobedience to God kicked off a terrible chain of events, resulting in the spiritual death of all mankind. Without divine intervention, we are doomed to eternal death, a spiritual and physical separation from God that never ends. But there is good news: Because God loves us, He wasn't willing to simply abandon us to death and destruction. He made a way to rescue us, and the Holy Spirit is a central part of that rescue plan. The Holy Spirit wants to breathe life into our dead spirits, reuniting us with God once and for all.

There is a very strange but enlightening passage in the book of Ezekiel, where God provides to the prophet a preview of

His rescue plan. Ezekiel wrote his book during a dire period of time in Israel's history. God's chosen people had disobeyed Him repeatedly, worshiping idols and violating His commandments. As a result of their sin, God banished them from the Promised Land and sent them into exile in the land of Babylon. Their physical separation from their homeland – and from the Temple where they worshiped God – was a vivid reminder that sin leads to estrangement from God, and eventually to death. The nation of Israel proved that they were no better than Adam and Eve by continuing the cycle of disobedience and death that began in the Garden of Eden. In fact, one of the saddest passages in the Old Testament is found in Ezekiel 10, when the Spirit of the Lord is seen departing from the Temple in Jerusalem. The nation is cut off from the life-giving presence of God's Spirit, and they are headed toward destruction.

In Ezekiel 37, though, the prophet wrote down a vision of what God promised to do in order to rescue His people from death. The Lord carried Ezekiel to a valley, where he saw piles and piles of human bones. If this sounds like the start of a horror movie, you understand the feel of the passage exactly right. The bones represented the Israelites, Ezekiel's doomed countrymen. They were spiritually dead, cut off from God's Spirit, and completely unable to bring themselves back to life. After Ezekiel saw the bones, God asked him a rhetorical question, "Can these bones live?" Ezekiel wisely replied, "O Lord God, You know!" The Lord then instructed Ezekiel to prophesy over the bones, to tell the bones that God was going to give them life again. So the confused prophet began to do what God asked, and the bones miraculously knit themselves together. Do you remember that old song about bones that you probably sang as a kid?

The foot bone connected to the leg bone,
The leg bone connected to the knee bone,
The knee bone connected to the thigh bone,
The thigh bone connected to the backbone,
The backbone connected to the neck bone,
The neck bone connected to the head bone,
Oh, hear the word of the Lord!

That song is actually about Ezekiel 37. And it describes exactly what happened when Ezekiel started to prophesy. All the bones connected together in just the right order. These dead bones turned into people with skin again. The only problem was that they still weren't alive. The valley of bones turned into a valley of reconstructed corpses. Impressive, yes, but still just a collection of skeletons.

God didn't leave His people in this state of living death, though. He told Ezekiel to command the breath, or the wind, to come from every corner of the earth in order to give life to these people. The prophet saw the wind blowing, and the people began to breathe. They stood on their feet, alive again. Those dry bones became living people again.

God finished this object lesson by telling Ezekiel that His Spirit can make dead people alive. Paraphrasing what God said, He told the prophet, "Ezekiel, even though these people are lifeless and hopeless, I will bring them back to life through the breath of My Spirit. I will raise them from the dead and give them a future in the land that I promised them" (Ezek 37:12–14). That is the power of God's Spirit. He brings dead people back to life. Dead people like you and me.

What it Means to Be Alive

American pop culture is full of stories about people who are functionally dead even though their bodies are technically alive. We call them zombies. Shows like "The Walking Dead" have popularized the zombie theme, and we seem fascinated with the concept of people who aren't really alive, but who can still chase you and eat you when they feel hungry. Many years ago, I saw the movie "I Am Legend," starring Will Smith. His character was the only normal person left in New York City after a terrible virus turned pretty much everybody else into dangerous zombie-like creatures. Their bodies were still alive, but it was like there were no lights on inside their brains. They didn't care about things like books, or movies, or friendship, or love. Their capacity for reason and emotion were destroyed; they lived only to survive. Will Smith's character eventually finds a way to bring these people back to life and make them normal again. He discovers a cure for the virus that has destroyed their minds and hearts, and these zombies once again become the human beings they were meant to be.

As we've seen in our discussion of the Holy Spirit so far, human beings who are separated from the life-giving power of the Spirit are like spiritual zombies. They are alive on outside, but dead on the inside. If that condition persists, their bodies eventually die also. That's why in Genesis 2:17, God warned Adam and Eve that on the day they ate from the Tree of the Knowledge of Good and Evil, they would die. I used to wonder what that meant; after all, they didn't drop dead the moment they took a bite from the forbidden fruit. But they died nonetheless. They chose the path of separation from God on that day and experienced the spiritual death that leads inevitably to physical death.

In order to be alive again, they needed to be reunited with the Life-Giver. For that to happen, somebody had to get rid of death once and for all. But since death is the just and irreversible consequence of our sin and disobedience, the penalty could not simply be waived. Someone had to pay it. That's where the gospel comes in: Jesus paid the penalty of death for us. He took upon Himself the death that we deserved, by dying on the cross. When Jesus rose again on the third day after His crucifixion, He proved once and for all that He had taken away the biggest barrier that keeps us from God. He put death to death.

Because Jesus defeated death, He paved the way for us to become alive again. Our spiritual resurrection happens when we believe in Jesus and the Holy Spirit regenerates us, or gives us a brand-new life. This was what Jesus meant when he told Nicodemus that he needed to be born again (John 3:3). The rebirth that Jesus described is accomplished through the Holy Spirit (John 3:5), who washes us clean from our sin and reunites us with God again. That reunification is what brings us back to life. No longer are we separated from God, on the pathway to physical and eternal death, but we are now alive again. The Holy Spirit lives within us (Romans 8:9–11), breathing life into our lifeless hearts. We are now on a trajectory toward physical resurrection, as well. Not even death can destroy the man or woman whom God has made spiritually alive. As Paul tells us in 1 Corinthians 15, one day Jesus will blow a trumpet, and everyone who is alive through the power of God's Spirit will rise from their graves. Jesus will bring new life, not only to His people, but to the world itself. We will experience the ultimate resurrection, reunited with God forever in a world that is free of sin, death, and Satan.

Before we go any further in our discussion of the Holy Spirit, then, ask yourself if you know Jesus. Have you ever trusted in Jesus Christ alone to forgive you of your sin and give you eternal life? If not, take a moment right now and tell Him that you want to accept the gift of eternal life that He is offering to you. Because Jesus died and rose again, you can know that He will give you life and a relationship with God that will never end. If you have believed in Jesus, then the Holy Spirit now lives in you. Through the Spirit, you have the ability to obey God in a way that you couldn't before you knew Him.

And if the Spirit of him who raised Jesus from the dead is living in you, he who raised Christ from the dead will also give life to your mortal bodies through his Spirit, who lives in you.

— ROMANS 8:11

What the Spirit Does Right Now

You might have read that previous section thinking, "Yes, of course I know that I'll go to heaven one day. I'm a Christian. But how does that help me right now?" Does the life-giving power of the Holy Spirit have anything to do with the sin, anxiety, division, and trouble that we experience today? In Chapter 1, I talked about many of the problems with the church today, and some of the ways in which we fall short of God's plan for our lives. Does the life provided by God's Spirit help us with any of those things *now*?

That question is what this book is about, and the answer is an unqualified and joyful, "YES!" Now that we have been resurrected by the power of the Holy Spirit, we can actually live like people who are, well, alive. We are no longer spiritual zombies. The Spirit of God not only revives us, but He promises to transform us. Through His power, we can become reflections of God's character, full of His love, truth, and righteousness. That's what will happen when we live Spirit-filled lives: We will know God in deeper ways, and we will increasingly reflect the character of Jesus Christ. His Spirit will change us from the inside out (Romans 8:5–8).

Here's the thing, though: In order to experience that type of transformation, we have to listen closely to the Spirit's voice. We must put ourselves in a position, day in and day out, where we can hear what He wants to tell us. And we must cultivate an attitude of submission and humility, so that we can see the ways in which we need be transformed. We are made spiritually alive in an instant as soon as we believe in Jesus; the Holy Spirit lives inside of every single Christian. But it takes a lifetime for us to become people who consistently *walk* in the power of the Holy Spirit. Over time, God wants us to form new habits and new attitudes, as we submit to the Spirit's transformation process.

Before we talk about *how* to develop those habits and attitudes, though, we need to look at the question of what we're aiming for. In other words, what does a Spirit-filled person actually look like? What changes should we see in our lives when we consistently breathe the air of the Holy Spirit? We will try to answer those questions in the next chapter.

REFLECTION QUESTIONS

1. Did you learn anything surprising about the Holy Spirit in this chapter?
2. Do you feel that you have a close relationship with the Holy Spirit? Why or why not?

CHAPTER 3

The Picture of Spiritual Health

"The Apostle does not speak of the works of the Spirit as he spoke of the works of the flesh, but he attaches to these Christian virtues a better name. He calls them the fruits of the Spirit."

— MARTIN LUTHER[11]

Before I was about 40 years old, I didn't bother to go to the doctor for my annual physical exam. I'm not recommending you neglect your own health in the same way, of course. But I rarely went to the doctor because I honestly felt just fine. Why would I spend good money just to hear the doctor tell me that I was a picture of physical health? As I have gotten older, though, I've become more diligent about seeing the doctor at least once a year. First of all, I have a family history of cancer, so yearly screenings are a good idea. Second, though, I don't always feel like the perfect picture of physical health anymore. My doctor gently reminds me that as I get older, my physical health won't stay on a permanent upward trajectory.

If you've ever had a routine physical, you know the drill. The doctor looks at all your bloodwork first, and lets you know of any areas of concern. Is your blood sugar alright? Any problems with your kidneys? Do you have anemia? These past couple of years, the doctor keeps telling me that my cholesterol is just a little bit too high. He politely threatens me with medication if I don't stop eating quite so many tortilla chips and blocks of cheddar cheese. I promise to do better in the future, but I usually go eat Mexican food after my appointment, as a way of comforting myself about the aging process. Growing older is uncomfortable. Everybody knows that our physical health declines as we age.

A doctor's job is to examine your health and compare it to a standard. If the baseline for a healthy cholesterol level is less than 200 and yours is 250, he will express concern. If your lungs should sound clear and full of air, but instead you're congested and short of breath, he will know there is a problem. In other words, the doctor has a picture of physical health in his mind, and he wants to see where you fall short. As much as it might feel like he's trying to hurt your feelings, his goal is to provide a pathway for you to be as healthy as possible.

Most of us have an idea of what physical health looks or feels like, but what about spiritual health? What is the baseline for a life that honors God? How do we know if we're spiritually well or spiritually sick? Before we can talk about the disciplines and habits that will help us to walk by the Spirit, we need to talk about the baseline for spiritual health. Here's the good news: While our physical health will probably decline the longer we're alive, our spiritual health can actually improve from year to year. We can be spiritually healthier at 80 than when we were 20, and we should be. But how will we know if we are healthier? What characterizes a Christian who is full of the Spirit's life-giving breath?

The Bible tells us that our character will change when we walk by the Spirit. We will begin to think, speak, and act in ways that are more like Jesus. The Bible also tells us that we will have the power to fulfill our mission, to make disciples as Jesus told us to do (Matthew 28:18–20). We'll return to the question of how the Spirit empowers our mission toward the end of this book. In this chapter, we are going to look at how the Spirit changes our character. There is no better place to start that discussion than with the famous "fruit of the Spirit" passage in Galatians 5.

The Fruit of the Spirit

We're going to take a deep dive into Galatians 5:22–23. There is probably no clearer passage in the New Testament describing the characteristics of a person who consistently breathes Spirit-filled air. However, many of us read the passage, and perhaps even memorize it, without pausing to think about it very much.

Before we look at each one of the nine characteristics in detail, though, we need to set the stage. First, this passage isn't a list of actions we need to do in order to earn God's approval. We'll talk about that more below. The important point to know for now, though, is that God has declared us completely righteous on the basis of our faith in Jesus (Romans 1:17). We can't earn God's approval by producing the fruit of the Spirit. Instead, the fruit of the Spirit is a list of attitudes, or character traits, which will increasingly mark our lives as we come to know God in deeper ways. These traits are a *response* to God's grace, produced by the power of God's Spirit. They are not a means by which we earn His acceptance. Our spiritual lives are rooted in grace from beginning to end.

It's also important to know that Galatians 5 follows Paul's extended discussion about why the Old Testament Law of Moses can never make us righteous. His basic argument is that the Law gave us rules to follow, but it didn't give us the power we needed to follow them. It showed us what God expected from us but still left us in a desperate situation. With the Law, we can see what God wants us to be, but we just can't seem to get there.

For those who believe in Jesus, though, the Holy Spirit changes the game. We now have the ability to obey God because God Himself lives inside of us. The main point of Galatians 5 is that we no longer have to be slaves to our sinful desires, because we have the ability to obey God through the power of the Holy Spirit. Here's the important thing to remember, though: We have to decide on a moment-by-moment basis whether we are going to obey the voice of the flesh or the voice of the Spirit. This isn't a once-for-all type of decision.

When Paul talks about the flesh, he is using that word as a sort of shorthand for a mindset opposed to God and His holiness. The flesh is the rebel who lives inside all of us, telling us that we can do whatever we want, whenever we want to do it, even if it violates God's will. In Galatians 5, Paul lists the character traits that result from listening to our flesh, and they aren't pretty (5:19–21). The list includes sexual immorality, jealousy, anger, strife, idolatry, drunkenness, and so on. It's a list that we see lived out in the world around us every single day. Sadly, it's a list we often see in ourselves.

Even when we try to do the *right* things, we seem doomed to fail. Trying to avoid sin without the Holy Spirit is like trying not to think about a white bear; the more you try to avoid it, the harder it becomes. For this reason, we often find ourselves defeated by our flesh, and unable to do the godly things we want to do (Romans 7). On the other hand, the result, or the fruit, of listening to the Spirit is love, joy, peace, patience, kindness, goodness, faithfulness, gentleness, and self-control. This is what naturally flows from listening to the Spirit's voice. Each moment, we have a choice whether to obey the flesh or to obey the Spirit. There are no other options.

"We will always experience conflict, whether we side with the Spirit against the flesh, or with the flesh against the Spirit . . . It is impossible for us to remain neutral; we either follow one or the other."
— THOMAS CONSTABLE[12]

There is No Easy Way

When my kids were small, they often resisted putting on their shoes whenever we left the house. Shoes are like kryptonite to small children. Most parents have experienced this baffling phenomenon. Children know that you're in a hurry, so they take a gamble that you'll let them go out barefoot rather than risk being late. If a parent routinely gives in to this sort of toddler terrorism, however, the behavior only increases. Like many parents, my wife and I would usually tell our kids something like, "Child, I realize that you hate your shoes with an irrational but very real passion. Nonetheless, you must put them on to go to church. We can do this the easy way or the hard way." The easy way consisted of the child willingly putting on her shoes. The hard way consisted of one parent holding the crying child while the other parent jammed the shoes on her feet against her will.

What I failed to realize at the time was that the easy way is a myth. There were only two hard ways. The way of obedience was hard, because our strong-willed child had to submit her will to her parents' authority. The way of rebellion was also hard, though, for more obvious reasons. And it was hard on parent and child alike. When we are forced to choose between submission and rebellion, there is no easy way.

Likewise, there is no easy way when it comes to our walk with God. There is no third option between listening to the Spirit and obeying the flesh. The way of the Spirit requires us to submit our will to God's authority. The way of the flesh leads us to estrangement from God. Both ways are hard, but only one way leads us to the life we really long for, a life of harmony with God and other people. Only the way of the Spirit leads us to a life of meaning and purpose. It's not an easy road, but it leads to a glorious destination. Paul put it like this in Romans 8:6, *"For the mind set on the flesh is death, but the mind set on the Spirit is life and peace."* Simple, yes; easy, no.

Attitudes not Actions

Now read Galatians 5:22–23, *"But the fruit of the Spirit is love, joy, peace, patience, kindness, goodness, faithfulness, gentleness, and self-control. Against such things there is no law."* Notice that the fruit of the Spirit is a list of *attitudes,* not actions. These attitudes originate in our minds and hearts, not in our actions. They will manifest themselves in our actions, of course, but Paul doesn't give us a list of rules here. He simply tells us what attitudes will characterize people who have a life-giving relationship with the Holy Spirit.

This is a huge change from the way most of us are accustomed to thinking about the spiritual life. We often make lists of behaviors that we think will turn us into spiritual people, or perhaps that will prove we already are. But healthy spirituality begins on the inside, not on the outside. The fruit of the Spirit itself isn't something we can *do* through our own willpower. Instead, the fruit of the Spirit is something we will naturally produce when we are breathing the Spirit's air.

> *"The branch cannot produce its own life; it must draw that life from the vine. It is our communion with Christ through the Spirit that makes possible the bearing of the fruit."*
> — WARREN WIERSBE[13]

"Fruit me!"

For just a moment let's look at another biblical metaphor for healthy spirituality. Psalm 1 describes a righteous person as a tree planted by flowing streams of water. Throughout the Bible, water is another image used for the Spirit of God. That's partly because the Holy Spirit washes us clean from sin, just like water washes dirt from our bodies. But like air, water also keeps us alive. Trees produce fruit only if they get enough water. A tree planted by flowing streams of water is going to bear much more fruit than a tree planted in the desert. It's basic biology.

Trees don't willfully make themselves produce fruit, though. You never see a tree wiggling its branches and shouting to the sky, "FRUIT ME!!" Instead, it simply sinks its roots deep into the ground and drinks as much water as possible. Its fruit is a natural consequence of being planted in the right spot.

Like trees, we can only produce spiritual fruit if we plant ourselves in the right spot, where the Holy Spirit's water can nourish us. In the next several pages, we are going to closely examine our lives to see if we are manifesting the fruit of the Spirit. But if we realize that we are falling short of God's desires for us, we aren't going to solve the problem with a list of rules designed to bring us back in line. Instead, we'll aim to put ourselves in a position to drink Spirit-filled water. The chapters that follow will examine some of the habits that will allow us to do just that.

Right now, let's look at the fruit of the Spirit one by one, starting with love. What attitudes will characterize us when we set our minds and hearts on the Holy Spirit? After a short discussion of each character trait, you'll find a list of questions to evaluate your own growth.

"It would have been enough to mention only the single fruit of love, for love embraces all the fruits of the Spirit."
— MARTIN LUTHER[14]

Love

Arguably the most popular love song of all time is Whitney Houston's performance of "I Will Always Love You," a song written by the inimitable Dolly Parton. In 1992, this song spent fourteen weeks at number one, and it remains one of the best-selling singles in history.[15] The combination of Dolly's sublime songwriting and Whitney's powerful singing makes it the type of song that people like to listen to over and over again. I love the song. I've always found it interesting, though, that the song's title is deceptive. The title would lead you to think the song is about undying love, the kind of love that never leaves even when times are tough (sort of like that Randy Travis classic, "Forever and Ever, Amen"). But "I Will Always Love You" is actually a break-up song. It's a "Dear John" letter from a person who is walking out the door but wants to encourage her wounded lover as she slams the door behind her. Sorry if I've ruined your childhood with my cynical take, but doesn't this song feel more like abandonment than love?

I think the song's lyrics tell us something important about our world's understanding of love, though. Love is seen as a feeling of affection that requires no endurance or real commitment. The world's version of love allows us to disengage – or even to leave – when the relationships get messy or inconvenient. Love as the world defines it is utilitarian. It's a love that perseveres so long as the object of our love gives us something in return, whether romance, sexual pleasure, prestige, or self-esteem. The world's version of love feels good for a period of time, but it doesn't reflect the love of God.

The word "love" in Galatians 5:22 is a translation of the Greek word "agape," which is the most commonly used word for love in the New Testament. Agape is the word the Bible uses to describe the love that God has for us, the love that we have for God, and the love that we have for one another. It can refer to any of those. Whichever relationship it refers to, though, the word agape always describes an active love. Agape isn't just a feeling, although feelings are involved. If I love Jesus, for example, I will keep His commands (John 14:15). If I love my wife, I will *give myself up for her*," much as Jesus did for us, sacrificing His own desires and rights so that we can flourish (Ephesians 5:22–33).

There are several passages in the New Testament where love is directly connected to the ministry of the Holy Spirit, and all of them highlight the active nature of His love. In Colossians 1:8, for example, Paul mentions that the church in Colossae was full of "*love in the Spirit,*" taking care of one another's spiritual and physical needs. In Romans 15:30, Paul invokes the love of the Spirit as a way of exhorting his friends to pray for him. And in Acts 2, the arrival of the Holy Spirit transformed the first Christians into incredibly generous people; they freely shared their homes and their possessions with one another (Acts 2:44). It's clear from these passages that the Holy Spirit is the One who fills our hearts with Christ's love, and who empowers us to actively care for the needs of other people.

Perhaps the most extensive description in the Bible of agape love is found in 1 Corinthians 13, famously known as the "love chapter." This chapter is often read at weddings, and it fits well in that context. But the love of 1 Corinthians 13 doesn't only apply to romantic love. It applies to all of our relationships. If I love somebody, Paul says, I will be patient and kind toward them. I will speak gently to them rather than rudely or arrogantly. I won't always insist on doing things my way. I won't rejoice when another person experiences injustice. I will always want what's best for them. I won't give up on people, but I will continue to believe that God is capable of transforming their lives just like He is transforming mine. I will be patient with others while they change and grow, just as I want them to be patient with me.

More than anything else, if I love somebody, I will want them to come to know Jesus in a deeper way. If they don't know

Him at all, then, I will tell them about Him. If they do know Him, I'll help them to know Him better. If there is some barrier keeping a person from obeying God, I'll help them remove that barrier. Agape love is active, not passive. Galatians 5:22 tells us that when we are connected to the Holy Spirit, our lives will be characterized by this active sort of love.

One way to tell if the love of Jesus is growing in our hearts is to ask whether we seek the best for people we don't really like very much. In the Sermon on the Mount, Jesus told His disciples to love their enemies and pray for people who persecuted them (Matthew 5:44). To be honest, this sounds like a pleasant enough idea until we actually have to do it. By definition, an enemy is somebody you don't feel like loving. Maybe your enemy is someone whose political views you find abhorrent. Maybe your enemy is a friend or a family member who said something terrible behind your back or even to your face. As hard as it is, being characterized by agape love means that we pray for our enemies. And we don't pray that God will curse them or destroy them. Instead, we pray that God will bless them and provide for them; after all, Jesus said, God causes the sun to rise on good and evil people alike (Matthew 5:45). He sends rain onto the fields of people who don't love Him. Jesus even died for His enemies so that they could have eternal life (Romans 5:8). In fact, we were once among those enemies. The gospel itself calls us to love those we might otherwise abhor, because Jesus did it first.

To be clear, love doesn't mean allowing yourself or others to be abused. Nor does love mean that we approve of everything another person does. Quite the contrary. Agape love means that I pray for God's best, even for people who say or do things that I *don't* approve of. I pray for people who hurt me, and for those who are far from God. Agape love calls me to engage with people I'd rather not know, and to be patient with people I'd rather give up on.

Be honest: Is that sort of love blossoming in your heart the longer you know Jesus? Or are you tangled up in anger and resentment toward your enemies? The Holy Spirit wants to fill our hearts with the agape love of Jesus. That can only happen, though, when we breathe the air of the Spirit on a momentary basis. Take a few minutes and read the questions in the box below. Answer them as honestly as possible and ask if your life reflects the love of Jesus.

AM I GROWING IN LOVE?

- Do I use my time and energy to help people know Jesus more closely?
- Do I listen to other people and give them the gift of my time and my presence, even when it is inconvenient?
- Do I pray for people even when I disagree with them or dislike them?
- Do I rejoice when my enemies experience pain, or do I want what is best for them?
- Do I forgive and persevere in my relationships, or do I give up on people when they disappoint me?
- Do I speak to people kindly, or are my words arrogant and rude?
- Do I insist on having things my own way, or do I set aside my own preferences and desires for the sake of other people?

Joy

One of the most famous organizational experts today is Marie Kondo, who hosts a show called "Tidying Up with Marie Kondo." Maybe you've seen it. Ms. Kondo helps people declutter their homes and recapture their lives by asking one simple question, "Does it spark joy?" The idea is to take everything in your closet, for example, and lay it on the floor. You touch each item and decide if it makes you feel a small internal spark of joy. If it does, then you keep it. If not, you need to let it go.

While I enjoy the show, I'll admit that I find Kondo's cleaning process a little bit silly. I'm much more likely to ask whether the item is something I need or not, even if it doesn't spark joy. I've never felt a special surge of joy from using a spatula, but I can't just throw them all away. I need them to make my scrambled eggs and hamburger patties.

Kondo's method, however, highlights an important reality of our lives: Even if something makes us happy today, it can lose its ability to make us happy tomorrow. We might have purchased a wonderful shirt three years ago, but now it's faded and out of style. Our new car feels exciting and joyful when we drive out of the dealership, but within a couple of years we long for a new one. Even more troubling, our relationships sometimes bring us more pain than joy. Marriage, childrearing, and work are all good gifts from God, but they don't always bring us the joy that we think they should. So how do we achieve the type of joy Paul describes in Galatians 5?

The answer is found in a number of New Testament passages about joy. The joy that Paul mentions in Galatians 5 springs from the unchanging promises of God. 1 Peter 1:3–6 (NASB), for example, describes the unfathomable blessings of eternal life:

*Blessed be the God and Father of our Lord Jesus Christ, who
according to His great mercy has caused us to be born again
to a living hope through the resurrection of Jesus Christ from
the dead, to obtain an inheritance which is imperishable
and undefiled and will not fade away, reserved in heaven for
you, who are protected by the power of God through faith for
a salvation ready to be revealed in the last time. In this you
greatly rejoice, even though now for a little while, if necessary,
you have been distressed by various trials.*

Our joy, Peter says, flows from hope. We have a hope that will
not fade away, unlike that new shirt or the new car. Biblical joy
comes from the reality that God has a plan to save us once and
for all. Nothing can take away that hope for those of us who
know Jesus.

What does this have to do with the Holy Spirit, though?
Jesus told His disciples that the Holy Spirit would remind them
of what He had taught them (John 14:26). When we are breathing the air of the Spirit, He constantly reminds us that we have a
joyful future because of Jesus. He constantly reminds us that we
have an inheritance that will always spark joy, even when everything on earth grows dull and joyless. Spirit-filled people have a
deep joy that the world can't remove from us, because the world
didn't give it to us in the first place. Do you possess that kind
of joy, the joy that comes from a life-giving relationship to the
Holy Spirit? Once again, honestly answer the questions about
joy that are in the box below.

AM I GROWING IN JOY?

- Do I remind myself on a daily basis of the joyful future that God has promised me through Jesus?
- Do I take daily joy in the reality that God loves me right now, just as I am?
- Do I allow my circumstances to overwhelm me and destroy my joy?
- Do I anchor my joy to Jesus, or to something else, such as how others treat me, how they think of me, my possessions, or my job?
- What situations in my life disappoint me and threaten to steal away my joy? Why?
- When I face those situations, do I pause to pray that the Lord will restore joy to me through the power of the Holy Spirit?

Peace

Most of us think of peace as an absence of war or conflict. As long as we aren't fighting somebody, we are at peace. The biblical concept of peace is much broader than that, however. In the Old Testament, the word "peace" is usually a translation of the Hebrew word "shalom." The New Testament was written in Greek, so Galatians 5 uses a different word, but it still refers to the same concept. Shalom is a hard word to translate well into English because it encompasses so much more than simply a lack of conflict. To possess shalom is to have a life in which all is well. It's a life where everything seems right with the world:

your relationship with God, your relationships with other people, and your expectations for the future.

You have probably experienced fleeting moments of shalom. Let me give you an example, If you are married with kids, imagine that your family is going on a vacation to the beautiful Rocky Mountains in Colorado. As you approach the mountains, you look out the window and find yourself in awe of God's creation. It feels like God Himself is smiling on you. You turn and look at your spouse contentedly; the two of you are getting along well during this trip, and so far, things are going just as you planned. The kids are in the back seat, and for once, they aren't arguing. They're talking to each other about everything they plan to do once you arrive at your destination, a sweet little mountain cabin where you will spend the next week, far away from work, school, and the normal routines of home. You are experiencing shalom at this moment. You're in harmony with God, harmony with the world, and harmony with your family. The future looks bright, at least for the next few days.

The problem, of course, is that such moments of shalom never last very long. Our circumstances can shift in a heartbeat. The kids start to argue and pull each other's hair. It starts to rain. Your car gets a flat tire. Your spouse begins to cry or to argue with you about how this vacation was a bad idea to begin with. The shalom balloon that you've been experiencing pops abruptly and painfully.

When Paul says that peace is a fruit of the Spirit, he's telling us that we can have a shalom, a fullness of life, that isn't rooted in our external circumstances. We can have harmony with God because Jesus died and rose again to give us peace with Him (Romans 5:1). As a result, the Spirit lives within us and provides us with an ongoing and never-ending relationship with

God. And because we are at peace with God, we now have the power to extend that peace to the people around us. Instead of a transient sense of shalom that comes from the circumstances around us, we have an eternal peace that flows from the inside out. Knowing our future is bright in the Lord brings us peace in the present moment. No matter what is happening around us, the Spirit of God provides us with an internal sense of peace that can never be shaken. However, we have to be listening to the Spirit's voice in order to experience that peace. We have to be filled with the Spirit in order to be full of shalom.

AM I GROWING IN PEACE?

- Is my relationship with God one of harmony, in which I willingly obey Him? Or do I find myself resisting Him and insisting on my own way of doing things?
- Are my relationships with other people harmonious and peaceful (e.g. my spouse, my parents, my roommates, my children, fellow Christians, co-workers, etc.)?
- Would other people describe me as a peacemaker?
- Do I have an internal sense of peace, rooted in the fact that God has given me a bright future through Jesus?
- When I feel anxious, do I turn my anxiety over to the Lord, trusting that He cares for me (1 Peter 5:7)?

Patience

Patience has never been my strong suit. I come from a proud tradition of impatience, in fact, especially as it pertains to driving.

My dad was a good driver, and a good driving teacher, but he had no patience for slow cars. I can still remember some of his advice from my early days of driving. "Hesitation produces accidents," he told me. "Son," he would say. "As soon as that light turns green, you press the gas pedal as fast and as hard as you can. Waiting for even half a second is inconsiderate to the vehicles behind you." There was also his belief that Cadillacs were the slowest cars on the road. He hated being behind slow drivers, and I have sadly inherited that impatience. And yet I live in a town where drivers routinely go well below the speed limit for no apparent reason. If the speed limit is 45 mph, for example, I often get stuck behind a car going 30. Few things can disrupt my connection to the Holy Spirit faster than a driver who won't pick up the pace.

Patience is a hard trait to cultivate because most of us hate waiting. What's more, we live in a culture that actively promotes impatience. We are accustomed to getting the answer to any question in an instant, simply Googling whatever we need to know. Previous generations labored over their meals for hours (or even days), but we can microwave our food in a matter of seconds. When I was a kid, we often sent people letters in the mail using stamps and envelopes. Today we call that "snail mail." We wonder why we'd even bother to write a letter on real paper, track down an envelope and a stamp, and wait several days for our message to arrive at its destination. It's so much faster to send a text message and receive an instant reply.

But when we read the Scripture, patience is a critical character trait for people who want to know God deeply. God has a pattern of asking people to wait, sometimes for decades, before He does something remarkable in their lives. Abraham waited until he was 100 years old before his son Isaac was born in fulfillment of God's promise. Moses waited for 40 years before God called him to deliver the Israelites. When Paul became a Christian, he spent three years in the desert, learning from God's Spirit and waiting for God to tell him what to do next. I could go on and on. Waiting is painful, but it's a critical aspect of the spiritual life.

Patience is a requirement for people who want to become holy. Patience is also an outcome of cultivating our connection to the Holy Spirit. It's one of the only character traits that is both an input and an output in the spiritual life. Walking with Christ will require patience while we wait for Him to speak to us. And the more we practice patience, the more patient we become.

AM I GROWING IN PATIENCE?

- Does being forced to wait make me feel angry, or can I remain calm and kind even when things are taking longer than I'd like?
- Am I willing to persevere in prayer, even when it seems like God isn't answering immediately?
- Do I listen to other people patiently, or does my attention span drift? Do I interrupt people if they take too long to make their point?
- Do I hurry people when they're moving too slowly, especially my family or those close to me?
- Am I patient with myself, trusting that God is transforming my character at His pace rather than my own?

Kindness and Goodness

My friend Blake is a car guy. If I hear a funny sound in my car, I call him before I even take it to the shop. If I need to buy a new car, I ask his advice before I turn to the internet. Blake doesn't merely understand cars, he loves them. While other people take Sunday afternoon naps, Blake takes Sunday afternoon drives. He buys classic cars that he knows he'll enjoy and works on them in his free time. For me, teaching a teenager to drive was terrifying, but Blake looks forward to the day when his kids reach that age. What could be more exciting than teaching your kids a skill that brings you such happiness?

A few years ago, Blake realized that his love for cars could help meet a serious need in our community. He realized that many people can't afford reliable vehicles. Without dependable transportation, it's hard for people to get to work on time, and therefore it's hard to keep steady employment. As a result, people without dependable cars often get stuck in a cycle of poverty.

Blake decided to start an organization, called OnRamp, to meet this need. With the help of generous donors, OnRamp gives away dozens of cars each year to people in need. It truly changes people's lives. Single moms are now able to find good jobs, get to work regularly, and support their families. What's more, his innovation has motivated other Christians to give away their used vehicles for free rather than trading them in or selling them.

OnRamp is an organization designed to spark kindness and goodness toward other people, as a reflection of the character of Christ. When Paul mentions kindness as a fruit of the Spirit, he's talking about that impulse to proactively seek what's best for other people. Goodness is a similar character trait; it probably refers more specifically to generosity. A kind or good person will notice a need, whether large or small, and seek to help. That help can be as simple as giving someone a glass of water when they're thirsty, carrying groceries for a person if they need help, or babysitting for free in order to give a young couple a few hours of rest. In Titus 3:3–5, Paul wrote that the ultimate expression of kindness was when Jesus saved us, forgave our sin, and gave us the Holy Spirit. He saw that we were in desperate need of mercy, and he took active steps to provide it for us.

Because the gift of the Holy Spirit is an expression of God's kindness, Ephesians 4:30–32 tells us that the Spirit is especially grieved when we're unkind to one another. When we are kind, though, we reflect the kindness of Jesus, and the Spirit rejoices. The better we come to know the Holy Spirit, then, the more we will be filled with the kindness that Christ modeled for us.

AM I GROWING IN KINDNESS/GOODNESS?

- Do you notice when other people around you are in need?
- Do you proactively seek to meet the needs of others, both small and large?
- Do you act kindly toward friends and foes alike, just as Jesus did?
- Are you kind to people who cannot repay you, or only to those who have something to give back?
- When was the last time you met a need for somebody without expecting anything in return?

Faithfulness

I find Proverbs 25:19 (NASB) to be one of the most vivid and memorable verses in the Bible: *"Like a bad tooth and an unsteady foot is confidence in a faithless man in time of trouble."* That image of a bad tooth really resonates with me. Children expect their teeth to fall out. My kids actually get excited about losing teeth, because they expect the tooth fairy (i.e. Mom and Dad) to give them some money for it. But adults are much less excited when their teeth fall out. For adults, unreliable teeth are a pain in more ways than one. Something as simple as eating an apple could lead to a painful dental procedure. Your teeth should be reliable and trustworthy, able to faithfully handle their chewing responsibilities.

Paul says that walking by the Spirit will make us increasingly faithful, more and more like good teeth. Spirit-filled people are dependable and trustworthy. They keep their word, even when it's hard to do. Faithful people don't bail out of their marriages, their responsibilities, or their faith as soon as times get tough. They show up, day after day, to read God's Word and to spend time in prayer. They don't give up on people, either, even when hope seems foolish.

Faithful people reflect the faithfulness of God. We worship a God who keeps loving us, even when we're unfaithful. The faithfulness of God is at the heart of the gospel, in fact, because Jesus promised that everyone who believes in Him will have eternal life. If Jesus isn't faithful, we can't trust that He will save us. He is faithful, though. The reality of His faithfulness is what motivated the writer of Hebrews to write, *"Let us hold fast the confession of our hope without wavering, for He who promised is faithful"* (Hebrews 10:23). We can remain faithful to God, because we know that God will always be faithful to us. He won't let us down. He promised us eternal life, and He will deliver.

The more regularly we breathe Spirit-filled air, the more we will come to understand and to reflect God's dependable, steady character. We will begin to recognize that keeping our commitments is one way to demonstrate how faithfully God keeps His. Marriage, for example, was designed to be an earthly reflection of God's love and faithfulness to His people (Ephesians 5:22–33). But we can also reflect God's character when we're faithful simply to do our jobs well or to finish our schoolwork on time. We can reflect His faithfulness when we do what we say we will do, even when circumstances make it difficult. Spirit-filled people are faithful in every area of their lives, even in a world where commitments are abandoned and promises are often broken.

AM I GROWING IN FAITHFULNESS?

- Do I keep my word, even when it costs me to do so?
- Do I honor my commitments (to my spouse, my job, my family, my friends) even when it would be easier to abandon them?
- Am I reliable? Can people depend on me to show up when I say I will and do what I say I'll do?
- Am I faithful in my spiritual life? Have I developed habits and disciplines to consistently grow in my walk with Jesus?
- Would other people in my life say that I am dependable or unpredictable? Am I more like a bad tooth or a solid rock?

Gentleness

When he was eight years old, my son started taekwondo training at a martial arts school in our neighborhood. The owners are slightly past middle age; this taekwondo school is a second career for them, one they dreamed about for a long time. The first thing I noticed and appreciated about the school was that the instructors expect respect from their students. Every question or command must be answered with an enthusiastic, "Yes sir," or "Yes ma'am." The students stand at attention in straight lines when they aren't actively practicing their techniques. Order and discipline are expected and necessary for students to succeed at the school.

I've also noticed, though, that the instructors create an environment of fun, even as they also cultivate respect. It's not at all unusual to see students sparring with each other while grinning from ear to ear. The trainers laugh with the kids and crack jokes to put them at ease. More importantly, they correct them with kindness and gentleness when their technique needs improvement, or when they make a mistake. Not once have I heard an instructor shout at a student or use an unkind word. Yet they still provide students with the feedback and correction that they need in order to get better. They tell the kids when they need to improve, and the kids listen because they know that their teachers only want what's best for them. Because of their patient yet firm instruction, my son trained at this school for many years, advancing all the way to black belt.

His taekwondo instructors are a good illustration of the gentleness Paul mentions in Galatians 5. Gentleness is a character trait that allows us to interact with other people kindly and humbly, even when we disagree. In 2 Timothy 2:25, Paul says that people who serve the Lord should be gentle when they correct their opponents. Notice he doesn't say they should ignore sin or approve of false teaching. Instead, he says that the Spirit-filled believer will address wrongdoing and error, but with humility and kindness. A gentle person is humble enough to know that he doesn't understand everything perfectly. He also realizes that shame and cruelty rarely create positive change in a person's life.

Just like the other fruit of the Spirit we've examined; gentleness reflects the character of God. God is gentle with us when we sin, even when we make the same mistakes over and over again (Numbers 14:8). He is patient with our spiritual immaturity, even when it takes us a long time to grow up. Jesus is the perfect example of gentleness because He perfectly reflects the Father. Jesus encouraged people to learn from Him, because He is *"gentle and lowly in heart"* (Matthew 11:29). In other words, Jesus isn't rough with us. He leads us and corrects us, but He does it patiently and kindly. The more we come to know Jesus, then, the more we will imitate His gentleness toward other people. When we breath in the air of the Spirit, we will begin to exhale gentleness as we interact with those around us.

AM I GROWING IN GENTLENESS?

- Am I eager to criticize and correct people, or am I sparing and wise with my critiques?
- When it is necessary to correct somebody, am I patient and kind?

- Do I raise my voice with other people, or am I calm and gentle?
- Do I choose words that communicate love and compassion, or am I rough with what I say?

Self-Control

One of the most famous psychology experiments of the 20th Century was the Stanford Marshmallow Experiment.[16] The researchers seated children between the ages of three and five years old at a table, on which they placed a marshmallow. The kids were then told that they could eat the marshmallow right away if they wanted. However, if they could wait for fifteen minutes, they would be rewarded with a second marshmallow. As you might imagine, some of the kids ate that first marshmallow immediately, figuring that one marshmallow right now is better than two marshmallows later. Others managed to wait, though. It wasn't easy for them, but they did it. First, they had to trust that the researchers were telling them the truth when they promised them a second marshmallow. Second, they had to take their minds off of the marshmallow right in front of them, in order to resist the temptation to eat it. Some kids distracted themselves by singing songs. Others looked at the ceiling. A few of the kids reminded themselves audibly that a second marshmallow was coming; they literally repeated the promise out loud.

Years later, the researchers found that kids who were able to wait for that second marshmallow were generally more successful at life. They had higher SAT scores and better grades in school. They were better at controlling their emotions in frustrating situations. They understood the concept of delayed gratification, which means setting aside pleasure right now in order to receive a better reward later.

That's the essence of self-control as the Bible defines it. Self-control doesn't mean living a joyless life, bereft of everything we like. Instead, self-control means that we learn to set aside the immediate desires of the flesh because we know that God has better things in store for us. For example, lashing out in anger feels good in the moment, but learning to control our anger will result in better relationships in the long run. Pornography provides immediate pleasure, but purity will lead to deeper connections with God and with our spouse. Scrolling social media can give us a short-term escape from the mundane realities of life but reading God's Word will result in much greater rewards in the long run.

Sustained self-control comes only from the Holy Spirit, not from our own willpower. In Galatians 5:19–21, Paul lists a number of actions that characterize those who simply follow their fleshly desires. Many of those actions are related to a lack of self-control: sexual immorality, rage, and drunkenness, for example. Apart from the Spirit's power, long-term self-control is virtually impossible. When we walk by the Spirit, though, we will learn to rely on His strength to resist temptation. We'll come to understand the eternal value of delayed gratification, and we'll constantly apply that understanding to our daily life.

Self-control is the final character trait on this list, but it is far from the least important. Learning to delay gratification is essential if we want to walk closely with God. Becoming more like Jesus is a slow process. It requires us to sacrifice our time and our desires to pursue something much greater, something that will last forever. It requires us to remind ourselves of God's eternal promises, day after day, month after month, and year after year. We have to trust that knowing Him deeply is worth the effort and the pain of spiritual transformation. That isn't easy to do, but we don't have to do it alone. The power of God's Spirit provides everything we need to keep our minds and hearts focused on His eternal promises.

AM I GROWING IN SELF-CONTROL?

- Is there a habit that has mastered me to the point that I cannot say "no" to it?
- When I am tempted to sin, am I able to resist the allure of short-term pleasure, trusting that God has better things in store for me?
- When I am tempted, do I stop and pray for God's help, or do I immediately rush into sin and then regret it later?
- When I honestly evaluate how I approach eating, speaking, sex, drinking, and other possible pitfalls, can I say that my life is marked by self-control?

Where We Go from Here

Now that we've looked at the fruit of the Spirit in detail, do you have a good idea of the areas in which you need to grow? If so, we need to figure out what it's going to take for us to move forward. How can we develop these attitudes in our lives in order to become more and more like Jesus?

As we've been saying all along, the answer to that question is for us to learn how to breathe properly. We need to cultivate a life-giving connection with the Holy Spirit on a day by day basis. In order to do that, we must develop regular practices that will lead us into the Spirit's presence. Some people call those practices "spiritual disciplines," but in this book we will simply call them spiritual habits, or spiritual breathing exercises. These habits will probably be familiar to you already. We'll be talking about things like Scripture meditation and study, worship, prayer, and community. We will see that a healthy spiritual life doesn't involve doing anything particularly novel or creative. Instead, it requires constantly practicing skills that are very basic, but that don't come naturally to us. In the next chapter, we will discuss the first of these skills. We'll examine how we can read and absorb God's Word in a way that will transform our hearts and produce in us the fruit of the Spirit.

REFLECTION QUESTIONS

1. After reading the descriptions of the fruit of the Spirit, where do you think you need the Spirit's transformation the most?
2. Are there any habits or attitudes you think you need to develop further in order to move forward in the areas where you're struggling?

CHAPTER 4

Breathing God's Word

"The Holy Ghost rides in the chariot of Scripture,
and not in the wagon of modern thought."

— CHARLES H. SPURGEON[17]

Your word is a lamp to my feet
and a light to my path.

— PSALM 119:105

In March 2016, a family in the southern United States was cleaning out an old house that had once belonged to their deceased great-grandparents. As they were throwing away old junk, they noticed a brown paper bag sitting on the floor. Curious, they picked it up and looked inside. What they found in that bag was both shocking and exhilarating. That grubby little package contained seven baseball cards, each with an image of the legendary center-fielder Ty Cobb. Despite having been on the floor of that old house for decades, the cards were in very good condition. The family submitted their find to several experts, who determined that the cards belonged to a very rare and valuable set that was printed between 1909 and 1911. Prior to this astounding find, only fifteen of these particular cards were known to exist. This was a once in a lifetime discovery, and it was a jackpot for this lucky family. The value of each card was estimated to be around $150,000, making the entire collection worth more than a million dollars.

I love stories like this. I like to imagine how I'd feel if I found an immensely valuable treasure hiding in my closet or my attic. I once found a one-hundred-dollar bill in the pocket of my suit coat, but that's about as close as I've come to that kind of windfall.

On the other hand, I have a priceless treasure sitting on my bedside table, one worth infinitely more than those baseball cards. I'm talking about the Bible, of course. In terms of eternal riches, God's Word is worth more than any other treasure on earth. Its pages contain the secrets of eternal life and the instructions we need in order to walk by the Spirit. Psalm 19 vividly illustrates the value of God's Word:

> *The law of the LORD is perfect, reviving the soul. The statutes of the LORD are trustworthy, making wise the simple. The precepts of the LORD are right, giving joy to the heart. The commands of the LORD are radiant, giving light to the eyes. The fear of the LORD is pure, enduring forever. The ordinances of the LORD are sure and altogether righteous. They are more precious than gold, than much pure gold; they are sweeter than honey, than honey from the comb. By them is your servant warned; in keeping them there is great reward (Psalm 19:7-11).*

There were few things in the ancient world more valuable than gold and silver. The Psalmist says, though, that not even gold and silver can match the value of God's Word. The Bible contains within its pages riches that will last for eternity, unlike any other riches we can accumulate in this lifetime.

If we want to learn how to breathe Spirit-filled air, we must learn how to read, study, memorize, and meditate upon the Scripture. It is one the most important tools that God uses to transform our hearts and teach us how to know and to obey Him. I've never known a truly godly person who wasn't regularly immersed in Scripture. We simply cannot become more like Jesus if we don't regularly breathe in His Word. There is no substitute for the living, breathing Word of God.

We said in the last chapter that cultivating a life-giving relationship with the Holy Spirit is simply a matter of regularly placing ourselves in a position where we can hear His voice. Breathing in the divine truth of God's Word is perhaps the most trustworthy way to habitually fill our minds and our hearts with the breath of His Spirit. Consider the reflection questions below as we begin our discussion of the Bible.

REFLECTION QUESTIONS

- How often do you read the Bible? Once a week? Every day?
- When you read it, do you feel that you are growing spiritually, or does it seem boring and lifeless to you? Why?
- What do you think would help you to grow in your ability and desire to read God's Word?

Cutting Deep

When I was a college student, I developed a painful lump on the sole of my foot one summer. My job required me to spend long hours standing on my feet, wearing uncomfortable dress shoes. For several weeks I ignored the pain, assuming it would eventually go away on its own. But it didn't. Instead, it got worse and worse, to the point that I had to sit down quite frequently and massage my own foot just to make it through the day. As you can probably imagine, this was embarrassing as well as uncomfortable. I finally made an appointment to have the foot examined.

I remember that the orthopedic surgeon was roughly six feet four inches tall, and his name was Dr. Small. Even more amusing, when he inspected my foot, he diagnosed me with a benign tumor commonly known as a "Morton's Neuroma." Yes, you read that correctly. I share a last name with the famous doctor who originally discovered this particular type of painful lump that was now growing on the bottom of my foot. Life is indeed stranger than fiction.

Unfortunately, my Morton's Neuroma was advanced enough that the only solution was surgery. Dr. Small used a local anesthetic, which meant that I was awake for the entire procedure. I wish I hadn't been. He cut the sole of my foot and extracted the neuroma. When I asked Dr. Small how I got this lump in the first place, he explained that something had irritated a nerve inside of my foot, causing excess tissue to grow and wrap itself around the injured nerve. Over time, the neuroma grew larger and larger. To cure me, the doctor had to cut me. He had to remove the damaged nerve along with everything around it.

In the same way, our hearts often grow hard spots, places where sinful attitudes and thoughts grow and become increasingly damaging to our walk with God. Just as my surgeon used his scalpel to remove that tumor, the Spirit of God uses the Scripture to cut away our sin and hard-heartedness toward God. Hebrews 4:12 (NASB) tells us,

> *"The Word of God is living and active and sharper than any two-edged sword and piercing as far as the division of soul and spirit, of both joints and marrow, and able to judge the thoughts and intentions of the heart."*

When we read the Bible, then, we will become aware of the ways in which we fall short of God's will for our lives. We'll start to see where our attitudes and actions reflect the deeds of the flesh more than the fruit of the Spirit, and we'll ask God to help us change.

When we make ourselves open to the Spirit's transformation, God won't leave us in a place of despair and hopelessness. God's Word only cuts us open in order to heal us. He doesn't show us where we fall short without leading us to spiritual transformation. In the words of 2 Timothy 3:16, *"All Scripture is God-breathed and is useful for teaching, rebuking, correcting and training in righteousness, so that the man of God may be thoroughly equipped for every good work."* The Scripture reveals our sinful hearts, but it also shows us how to change.

The word "God-breathed" in 2 Timothy 3:16 isn't found anywhere else in the Bible. The apostle Paul apparently made this word up just to describe the power of the Scripture. He's saying that the Holy Spirit, the living and active breath of God, is responsible for giving us God's Word. God breathed it out so that we can breathe it in. And when we do breathe it in, the Scripture changes us. We become people who are wise, fruitful, righteous, and ready for whatever God might call us to do.

I think most Christians would agree that the Bible is necessary for their spiritual growth. Consider the following statistics from a survey conducted by the Barna Group: 79% of Americans consider the Bible to be sacred, containing the very words of God. 88% of Americans own at least one Bible, and on average each of us owns three of them. However, only 37% of us read the Bible even once a week. Only 15% of us read it every day.[18] Another survey found that only 20% of Americans have read the entire Bible; most have only read a few passages or stories.[19] In other words, we say that the Scripture is God's Word, and we believe it is extremely important and valuable. We just don't read it.

The reason we don't read the Bible probably has more to do with a failure to develop the right habits than with any doubts we have about the value of God's Word. Remember, learning to breathe Spirit-filled air is a matter of consistently placing ourselves in a position where we can hear the Spirit's voice. When it comes to the Bible, that means we need to structure our time and our routines so that we can consistently breathe in the Word that God's Spirit has breathed out. For the rest of this chapter, we will talk about those habits and how to build them into our lives.

Finding Time to Read

When I was in my early 20s, I was in an extremely busy season of life. At least, it was the busiest I'd ever been. I was on staff at my church, working as an intern for the college ministry. To make ends meet, I also worked a second job at a local print shop. I spent time with my friends and roommates, I tried to pray and read my Bible regularly, and I occasionally found time to call my parents so they'd know I still loved them. If you'd asked me to join a club or lead a committee, I would have told you that I didn't have time. My calendar was full.

But then I met a beautiful young woman named Shannon and asked her out. Within a few weeks, we were spending almost all of our free time together, from the time we both got off work each evening until about midnight. It was amazing how I suddenly had more free time than I'd previously dreamed possible. It turns out that I wasn't too busy to make time for something that was truly important to me, which was wooing the woman who eventually became my wife.

We all make time for the things that matter to us. If staying healthy is important to you, you'll find some time to exercise. If you want to have good relationships with your kids, you'll find the time to spend with them. Reading the Bible is no different; if it's truly important to us, we will find time to read it.

Where can we find that time, though? Like most people, I struggle to find a consistent time to read the Bible. If I don't make it a priority, life gets in the way. That said, consistency isn't impossible; we just have to be a bit creative. When my kids were very young, they often woke up so early that I couldn't find any time in the morning to read. So I read in the evenings instead. Now, evenings are busier for our family than they were back then, so I read my Bible in the morning. You will need to consider your own schedule carefully in order to find available time slots. You don't necessarily need a lot of time, by the way. If you can devote about fifteen minutes each day to Scripture reading, you can probably read the entire Bible in the course of year. Almost all of us have fifteen minutes to spare.

We also have modern tools that previous generations didn't have, tools that make finding time a bit easier. For example, there are smartphone apps that let you use your daily commute to listen to the Bible in your car (YouVersion, for example). In fact, I often listen to the Scripture on my way to the office. Throughout history, more people have listened to Scripture than have read it themselves, especially since reading has not always been a common skill. In fact, I find that I notice things when I listen to the Bible that I might otherwise miss when I read it to myself. Whether you read or listen, though, the goal is to find time on a consistent basis to engage with God's Word. The habit itself is more important than the manner in which you accomplish it.

EXERCISE: FINDING TIME TO READ THE BIBLE

Before we move to the next section, take a few moments right now to look at your daily calendar. See if you can find a consistent time to read the Bible. Maybe you can get up fifteen minutes earlier in the morning, or retire to your bedroom a few minutes early each night to read. Maybe you can read while you eat lunch. Years ago, I even heard about one man who realized that he spent nearly an hour each day in stop-and-go traffic on his way to work. He decided that when the traffic was stopped, he would read his Bible. If reading God's Word truly matters to you, you can find a time to do it.

Reading the Bible is Different

Since you're reading this book, I think it's safe for me to assume that you're a literate person. It might seem strange (and perhaps a bit offensive) for me to suggest that you need to learn how to read the Bible. However, the Bible is quite a bit different from other books. It takes a good deal more effort and time to understand the Scripture than it does to understand the latest John Grisham novel. There are a few reasons for this.

First, the Bible was originally written thousands of years ago, to people living in societies much different from our own. For example, the world of the Bible was much more agrarian than our own. As a result, there are lots of stories and metaphors about things like wheat and sheep, subjects that most of us don't know much about these days. Most societies were patriarchal, meaning that the father had a great deal more power and authority in the family structure than we're accustomed to seeing today. Most people couldn't read, also, so large portions of the Bible were written in order to be read aloud, or even sung. There are customs and traditions in the Scripture that sound quite strange to us but were completely normal at the time.

Second, the Bible has been translated, mostly from Hebrew (in the Old Testament) and Greek (in the New Testament). While you don't need to know these languages in order to benefit from reading the Bible, it's helpful to know that different English versions of the Bible might translate things slightly differently. Some versions tend to be much more literal than others, like the New American Standard. Other versions are more like paraphrases, like The Message. What's more, some biblical words are notoriously difficult to translate into English. In the book of Ruth, the Hebrew word *hesed* is extremely significant.

It's not a word that is easy to translate; it can mean "loving-kindness," "faithfulness," "loyalty," "mercy," or "graciousness," depending upon the context. It often refers to God's faithful, loyal love—the kind of love that always keeps its promises and commitments. It's an incredibly rich word, and sometimes English versions don't quite capture its power. These language barriers can make reading and understanding the Bible in English difficult at times.

Third, the Bible deals with difficult and complicated issues related to God. I vividly remember sitting at Taco Cabana with my kids one evening, peacefully enjoying my tacos, when my kids started peppering me with questions about whether God has a beginning, where Satan came from, why God doesn't kill him right now, and if God actually died when Jesus was crucified. I was tempted to tell them to just be quiet and eat their little quesadillas, but instead we talked about how the Bible sometimes raises as many questions as it answers for us, and how that can be frustrating to those of us who like clear solutions to every problem.

Fourth and finally, the Bible is a divine book. It wasn't written merely to educate us, but to transform us. Unlike any other book in the world, we can't read the Bible like detached observers and expect it to do what it's meant to do in our hearts. As soon as we start reading it with open hearts, the Holy Spirit is going to start working on us. That's often going to feel painful and convicting, rather than enjoyable. For that reason, reading the Bible doesn't merely stretch us intellectually, but spiritually and emotionally, as well.

In the face of these challenges, many people simply give up. Many yearlong Bible reading plans meet their tragic deaths in the book of Leviticus, a book that is particularly difficult for modern readers. The cultural, linguistic, and theological challenges pile up, and it's easy to get discouraged and wonder why you should try at all. I want to exhort you not to give up, though. We really can get better at reading and understanding the Bible. It won't be easy, and it won't happen overnight. But growing is a matter of consistent practice, and of using the tools and resources at our disposal.

Practice Makes Progress

Allow me to make a confession that might cause you to think less of me: I didn't really enjoy teaching my children to read. The outcome is worth the effort since reading is a critical life skill. But listening to small children read can be excruciating. I remember sitting on the sofa with each of my kids waiting for them to sound out simple words like "cat" or "bug." Each word took at least five or ten seconds to read, since they sounded out the words one letter at a time. When your kids' teacher asks you to listen while your child reads a book with 250 words, every one of which is a struggle for them, reading tends to lose its luster. I'm not sure who cried more during those early reading lessons, the kids or me! With daily practice, though, they got better. By the grace of God, all three of my kids are proficient readers today, and they actually enjoy it! Apparently, the trauma of plowing through terrible books with titles like, "Bill Got a Dog" didn't completely destroy their love of the written word. Practice makes progress, and eventually it leads to proficiency.

That same principle holds true when it comes to reading the Bible. Practice makes progress. If we want to learn how to read the Bible well, we must start reading it regularly. Let me encourage you to develop a habit of reading the entire Bible on a yearly, or semi-yearly, basis. As I mentioned before, it's fairly easy to pull this off if you allot about fifteen minutes a day. There are literally hundreds of Bible-reading plans online for you to choose from.[20] I personally use one that requires me to read only five days a week, because I know myself well enough to realize that I'll probably miss some days here and there. If the entire Bible sounds like too much for you, start with the New Testament and then move on to the book of Psalms. Whichever plan you use, just start reading, day in and day out.

Your goal is simply to breathe in the written word of God on a daily basis. As you do, you'll find that your mind will increasingly turn toward the Bible when you face challenging circumstances and complicated decisions. In those moments of pressure, when you might otherwise display the deeds of the flesh, the Spirit will speak to you and show you a better way. Your responses and attitudes will be characterized more and more by the fruit of the Spirit. You'll be amazed at how God's thoughts will fill your mind when you saturate yourself in His word.

Conviction Leads to Transformation

Many years ago, I was reading my Bible when I read a story about King David that unexpectedly changed my life. If you're familiar with the story of David's life, you'll remember that God chose him to become the next king of Israel when he was a relatively young man (1 Samuel 16). Because of King Saul's disobedience, God decided to replace him with David, a leader famously described as a *"man after God's own heart"* (1 Samuel 13:14). That doesn't mean that David was perfect, but it does mean that he faithfully and humbly obeyed God.

However, several years passed between the time that David was anointed and the time that he actually became king of Israel. During those years, King Saul repeatedly attempted to kill David, at one point even hurling a spear at him to pin him against the wall (1 Samuel 18:10). David had to flee to the wilderness, where he lived in hiding until King Saul died.

Once, during that time period when David was on the run, he had an opportunity to kill King Saul and to claim the throne of Israel for himself (1 Samuel 24). After an exhausting day of pursuing David through the desert, Saul had to go potty (that's my rough translation of the Hebrew text). By a remarkable coincidence, Saul chose to relieve himself in the very same cave where David and his men were hiding. Saul didn't see David's men inside the cave, but David's men saw Saul. So David snuck up behind the king and cut a tiny little corner off of his robe.

Cutting the corner off of someone's robe doesn't sound like a big deal, to be honest. In fact, I've always felt that David exercised amazing restraint by not killing that cruel king on the spot. But David felt guilty about it, nonetheless. He knew that it was wrong to lay a finger on the king of Israel, even to cut a piece of fabric from his robe. Only God had the right to stretch out his hand against the ruler of Israel, and David knew that he wasn't God. His conscience was deeply troubled by this seemingly insignificant violation of God's holiness.

As I read that passage one morning, the Holy Spirit suddenly convicted me in a profound and painful way. He reminded me of an episode in my own life in which I'd acted dishonestly toward another person. It was a small act of dishonesty, much like what David did to Saul; the other person would never know what I'd done unless I told him. But telling him was exactly what the Spirit was convicting me to do in that moment. I tried to ignore those feelings of conviction, but they wouldn't go away. I confessed my sin to the Lord, but I knew that I needed to confess directly to the person I had sinned against. So, I wrote him a letter and told him what I'd done. I expected that my confession would ruin our relationship or even cause damage to my reputation. But in that moment, I cared more about restoring my relationship with God than I did about my reputation.

God was kind to me that day, even though the Spirit's conviction was painful. As it turned out, the other man wrote me a very kind letter in response, extending his forgiveness and telling me not to worry about the incident anymore. But even if my friend hadn't been so forgiving, I wouldn't regret sending him that letter. As soon as I made the decision to do the right thing, I felt an enormous weight lift from my heart. The Spirit cut me open, but only in order to make me more like Jesus.

Friends, that's the power of breathing in God's Word. The Scripture will cut you open, but it will also heal you. In order to experience that type of transformation, though, we need to learn how to read and study God's Word deeply. That will take time and effort, but the investment is more than worth it.

How can we make that investment count, though? Before we close this chapter, I want to talk about a few skills to help us make the most of our time in God's Word: study, meditation, and memorization.

"The Bible was not written to satisfy your curiosity but to help you conform to Christ's image. Not to make you a smarter sinner but to make you like the Savior. Not to fill your head with a collection of biblical facts but to transform your life."
— HOWARD HENDRICKS[21]

Learn to Study

Bible study is a bit of a divisive subject. If you're a brainy sort of person, you might love digging into the details of a passage to know as much as possible. You're the type of person who belongs to three weekly Bible studies and you're always the smartest one in the room. On the other end of the spectrum are those who have an allergic reaction to the word "study." Maybe Bible study reminds you too much of your middle school grammar class, and that's a period in your life that you'd rather forget.

The goal of Bible study, though, isn't to fill our minds with facts so that we can impress our friends and neighbors. We study the Bible because the more we know about God and His Word, the better we're able to obey His will for our lives. In other words, we study the Bible in order to apply it correctly.

Once we've developed a daily habit of *reading* God's Word, we can increase our understanding by learning how to *study* it in a deeper way. The beauty of the Scripture is that we could read it and study it for our entire lives and never reach a point where there is nothing more to learn. Because it's a divine book, there's always something more we can learn about God, no matter how many times we've read it.

If you want to learn how to study the Bible, I strongly recommend picking up a copy of *Living by the Book,* written by the legendary seminary professor Howard G. Hendricks. Hendricks helpfully breaks Bible study down into three tasks: observation, interpretation, and application. Each step in the Bible study process is designed to help you gain a better understanding of God's Word, so that you can more faithfully obey God. In Appendix 1, I've included a basic guide to this process of Bible study to help you get started.

Much like learning to read, Bible study is a skill that takes practice and dedication. If you're already in the habit of reading the Bible for 15-30 minutes each day, work on adding some time into your calendar to study it more deeply. You might not do this every single day, but perhaps you have an extra hour on the weekend, or one evening a week, where you can pull out a pen and a notebook and spend a bit more time learning from Scripture.

If you'd like some resources to get you started, Grace Bible Church in College Station, Texas (where I serve as a pastor) has a number of Bible studies designed to help you with this skill. I'd recommend starting with our study on the book of 2 Timothy. It's short, relatively easy to understand, and 2 Timothy centers on the concept of making disciples. Go to www.grace-bible.org/resources and you'll find a free download in the Curriculum section of the website. Learn to study the Bible and you'll open up a whole new world of spiritual understanding.

REFLECTION QUESTIONS

- Does Bible study intimidate you? Why or why not?
- Is there a Bible study in your local church or community that you would consider joining right now?

Meditate

As a kid growing up in church, I remember being warned about meditation. Meditation was a weird and scary habit, something practiced by Hollywood actors who sat in a lotus position while reciting ancient Hindu mantras. Perhaps because of the fear that meditation is too closely connected to Eastern religion, I've rarely heard of a pastor encouraging his congregation to meditate.

The Bible does encourage God's people to meditate on His Word, though. In Psalm 1:2, the blessed man meditates on God's law, "*day and night.*" Psalm 119, the longest chapter in the Bible, includes at least six references to the importance of meditating on God's Word. In Philippians 4:8, Paul tells his readers to "think" about things that are true, noble, right, pure, and so on. The Greek word he uses in that passage is one that has the idea of carefully pondering or reflecting upon certain things. In other words, we're called to meditate on what is true, and what greater truth is there than the Word of God?

Biblical meditation is quite different from Buddhist or Hindu meditation, however. The goal of meditation in Eastern religions is to empty the mind of all thoughts, desires, or opinions. The goal of biblical meditation is to *fill* our minds with the truth of God's Word. What we're hoping to do when we meditate on Scripture is to replace our sinful and fleshly thoughts with the holy and spiritual thoughts of God.

How do we meditate on the Scripture, then? We begin by reading a passage repeatedly. Read it aloud and not merely inside your mind. Saying something out loud engages not only our minds in the act of meditation, but also our bodies. It also helps us with memorization, which we will discuss more below. As you read the passage, turn the words over in your mind. Think about them carefully. Formulate questions and answer them as well as you can. For example, imagine you're reading Psalm 1:1: "*Blessed is the man who does not walk in the counsel of the wicked or stand in the way of sinners or sit in the seat of mockers.*" After you read it aloud several times, you might ask yourself, "Why is there a progression of movement in this verse, from walking, to standing, to sitting?" Or, "What does it mean to be blessed?"

Remember, you aren't necessarily studying the passage right now; you're just pondering it, chewing on it in your mind, and allowing the Spirit of God to speak through its words. You're letting God's Word saturate your heart and mind so that it becomes a part of you. As it does that, the Spirit will begin to transform the way you think. Your values will slowly align with the values of God. Fleshly thoughts – anger, lust, pride, greed, envy, and the like – will slowly be replaced with spiritual thoughts and feelings. It isn't an immediate transformation but meditating on Scripture is a powerful step in the process of learning to breathe God's Word.

EXERCISE

Spend 5-10 minutes meditating on 2 Timothy 3:16–17. Ask God for wisdom. Read the verse aloud 4-5 times, carefully pondering each word. Ask yourself questions like, "What would it look like for me to be complete, and equipped for every good work?" Finish by asking God to help you obey Him, through the power that His Spirit provides.

Memorize

When I was a young adult, I had a roommate named Tim, who had an unbelievable ability to memorize Scripture. I can remember him reciting entire chapters of the New Testament with ease, while I struggled to keep even one or two verses in my brain. Even more remarkable, Tim could tell you the location of almost any passage in the Bible with stunning accuracy. We often tried to stump him by reading verses from books like Obadiah or Zephaniah and asking him to tell us where in the Bible they were. Most of the time, Tim could get at least the book right, if not the chapter and verse. I never had the same ability to recall information that Tim did. As a result, I often didn't try. Like many people, I told myself that I wasn't really that good at memorizing the Bible.

Something changed, though, during my first year in seminary. First-year students were given an assignment in which we had to write down a single verse from the book of Philemon, over and over again, in order to study it carefully. One day in class, I suddenly found myself able to recite the passage from memory, even though I wasn't actively trying to memorize it. I realized that being able to memorize a verse is quite often simply a function of reading it repeatedly. Reading it aloud is better than reading silently. And if you can write the passage down, that's even better; something about writing assists with our ability to recall information. By my third year of seminary, I memorized the entire book of Philippians using this method. I read the book in small sections (1-3 verses at a time), over and over and over, until my mind could recall each section. Then I just pieced them together slowly over the course of a few weeks.

Memorization isn't a magical skill, nor is it inaccessible to most people. It's a matter of diligence and patience. And the payoff is worth the effort. I've found over the years that verses from Philippians often come to my mind at critical moments. I believe that the Holy Spirit reminds me of them when I need to remember. When I'm struggling with anger or bitterness toward another person, I suddenly recall Philippians 4:8: *"Finally, brethren, whatever is true, whatever is noble, whatever is right, whatever is pure, whatever is lovely, whatever is admirable, if anything is excellent or praiseworthy, think about these things."* When I have to clean up the dishes more often than I think is fair, I remember Philippians 2:14–15 (NASB): *"Do all things without grumbling or disputing, so that you will prove yourselves to be children of God, above reproach in the midst of a crooked and perverse generation, among whom you appear as lights in the world."*

Writing God's Word on your heart changes the way you think, feel, and act. Having the Scripture committed to memory is one of the most powerful ways that we can put ourselves in a position where the Spirit can transform us. When you're memorizing the Bible, you are definitely breathing life-giving air.[22]

EXERCISE

Read Galatians 5:22–23 aloud as many times as you can in 10 minutes. Then see how much of it you can recite from memory, without looking at your Bible. Have your spouse or a friend check it for you. Keep trying until you can recite the fruit of the Spirit from memory.

Keep Showing Up!

Like any discipline in life, reading and studying the Bible takes consistency and practice. At first, you might struggle with the words and concepts. Your attention span might drift while you read, and you'll wonder if this is worthwhile. For many people, they give up when they run into Old Testament books like

Leviticus, which don't seem to have a great deal of immediately applicable content.

The greatest tip I can give you, though, is to just keep showing up. Remember, our goal is to put ourselves in a position where we can hear the Spirit's voice, day in and day out. The only way to accomplish that is to simply build a habit of saturating ourselves in the Word of God. As we said in the beginning of this book, the process of spiritual formation isn't easy, and it takes a lifetime, but it's worth it. Learning to engage with the Word of God is a critical step in that process of becoming more like Jesus.

As we read God's Word and come to know Him better, we will find ourselves wanting to worship Him more and more. In our next chapter, we'll talk about another practice that will fill us up with the air of God's Spirit: singing praises to the Lord.

REFLECTION EXERCISES

1. After reading this chapter, what is one specific way you can improve when it comes to reading and applying God's Word?
2. Consider using the resource, "52 Memory Verses Arranged by Topic" as a way to commit more Scripture to memory over the course of the next year.

CHAPTER 5

Habits of Praise

*Praise the Lord! For it is good to
sing praises to our God; for it is
pleasant and praise is becoming.*

— PSALM 147:1 (NASB)

My church is in College Station, Texas, the home of Texas A&M University, where I also went to college. Texas A&M students are called "Aggies," and there is a whole subgenre of jokes dedicated to making fun of our supposed stupidity. Aggies complain about the jokes, but we secretly love them. In fact, the best Aggie jokes are usually created in-house, by clever and self-deprecating A&M students.

The school was founded in 1876, and it's known for its rich traditional culture. There's a joke that if something happens twice at A&M, it becomes a tradition. That's not far from the truth. Incoming students attend Fish Camp, a week-long introduction to the history and traditions of the university. They learn about the Corps of Cadets, yell leaders, Aggie rings, Elephant Walk, special hand signs called "wildcats," songs to sing during football games, and why they shouldn't walk on the grass outside the Memorial Student Center. There are elaborate rituals and traditions for almost everything that happens on campus.

If you ever go to an Aggie football game, you might think you've stumbled into some sort of extremely friendly cult. Everybody wears the same clothes, sings the same songs, and chants in unison. Aggie fans wrap their arms around each other and sway back and forth while they sing. In fact, this whole-hearted devotion to Aggie culture extends beyond football games, into regular life. Once you're an Aggie, you're always an Aggie, even if you graduated 80 years ago. I actually knew a man who played a recording of the Aggie War Hymn (the school fight song) in the delivery room, while his wife was giving birth to their first child. It can all feel like a bit much to people who aren't on the inside.

It's not too much of a stretch to say that this devotion that Aggies demonstrate toward their school is a form of worship. Don't get me wrong: Very few Aggies would say that the school is actually their god (although some might, if they're being honest). But when I say that Aggies engage in worship, I mean they believe that A&M is worth their time, their money, their energy, and their affections. Aggies sing songs about A&M to proclaim how great it is. They spend money on clothes, classes, and tickets because it's worth it to them. Aggies even evangelize! Ask any Aggie why somebody would want to go to A&M, and you'll hear a sermon about why it's the best place on earth. I love my alma mater, but I also understand why people think it's a strange religion.

Everybody Worships Something

Everybody worships something or somebody. When we worship something, we declare that it's worth our time, our energy, our affections, and our resources. Worship proclaims that the object of our worship is valuable. A lovestruck poet might say to his beloved, "I worship the ground you walk on." He's saying that she's wonderful; she's worthy of everything her lover can give her.

If we worship God, then, we're saying that God is worthy of everything we can give Him. We worship God when we sing songs of praise, when we give money toward His purposes, or when we serve His people. When we worship God, we set Him at the very top of our life's priority list, ahead of everyone and everything else.

Worship is one of the main ways that the Holy Spirit speaks to us. In fact, the Bible says that when we worship God, His Spirit fills our hearts in a powerful way! Singing praises, giving thanks, and serving others are means through which God fills us with His spiritual breath. In this chapter, we're going to focus primarily on singing, because it's mentioned so often in Scripture. The thought that singing is one of the best ways to connect with the Holy Spirit might seem strange to you, especially if you aren't musically inclined. But it's amazing how frequently the Bible commands us to sing praises to God. It's no exaggeration to say that if we want to be filled with the life-giving breath of God's Spirit, we *must* sing. In Ephesians 5:18–21, Paul directly connects singing to being filled by the Holy Spirit:

Do not get drunk on wine, which leads to debauchery. Instead, be filled with the Spirit. Speak to one another with

> *psalms, hymns and spiritual songs. Sing and make music*
> *in your heart to the Lord, always giving thanks to God the*
> *Father for everything, in the name of our Lord Jesus Christ.*
> *Submit to one another out of reverence for Christ.*

This passage uses a particularly vivid analogy to describe what the Holy Spirit does when we sing praises. Paul tells us that instead of being drunk on wine, we should be filled with the Holy Spirit. Most of us have seen drunk people, even if we've never been drunk ourselves. When a person drinks too much alcohol, it controls them. Their thoughts, their words, and their attitudes are deeply affected by it, to the point that we might say, "Oh, that's not really Tom speaking. It's the whiskey." It's probably more accurate to say that it is, in fact, Tom speaking. It's just a version of Tom that is being heavily influenced by an external power, which just happens to be whiskey.

When someone is drunk, they're not fully in control of their faculties. Most of what people do under the influence of alcohol isn't good, and it might not be consistent with how they act in everyday life. They're still responsible for their actions, though, and for the choice to start drinking in the first place. For that reason, Paul says we should avoid getting drunk with wine.

What's more important here, though, is that he says that we should be filled with the Spirit of God instead. Paul doesn't merely tell us what to avoid; he tells us what to pursue. There's a bit of a play on words here: *"Don't be filled with the spirits [wine] but be filled with the Spirit."* In other words, if you're going to be controlled by something, be controlled by the Holy Spirit. If you're going to allow something to enter into your mind and your heart, to direct your thoughts and actions, make sure that it's the life-giving breath of the Holy Spirit, and not the life-destroying liquid of alcohol.

What happens when we choose to be filled with the Spirit? Paul tells us right there in the text: Spirit-filled people sing praises to God. Scholars debate whether singing praises is a result of being filled with the Spirit, or a means by which we become filled with the Spirit.[23] At the risk of sounding like I'm copping out, I'm going to suggest that the answer here is both. When we're consistently breathing the air of God's Spirit, we're going to respond to Him by singing praises. But it's also true that when we worship God in song, we're taking deep spiritual breaths, filling our hearts with His Spirit. So, singing is both a result and a means of being filled with the Holy Spirit. For that reason, it's one of the most powerful spiritual disciplines available to us, but it's also one of the most frequently overlooked.

"Music speaks of universal things. Common experience. That's why your lungs swell and your eyes close and you force as much air as possible through your vocal cords whenever you encounter a song that expresses what is your life."
— DAVID CROWDER[24]

Habits of Worship

One afternoon I was driving down the road when one of my favorite songs came on the radio. Like many people in that situation, I began to sing along. I don't remember what song it was, but I remember that it was upbeat and fun. The more I sang, the more animated I became. When I stopped at the next light, I started to dance just a little bit. It's possible that I even pretended I was holding a microphone like a rock star as I sang into the air. It was all very impressive.

What I didn't notice was the young couple in the car next to me. They saw my song-and-dance routine and found it quite amusing. By the time I looked over at them, they were laughing so hard they were crying. I hadn't even considered whether anybody else could see me singing, and I was embarrassed when I saw them laughing at me.

That's the power of music, though. It has a way of filling our hearts and our minds completely. It can even make us move our bodies; we've all had the experience of suddenly noticing that our body is swaying in time to our favorite pop song. That's why Paul says in Ephesians 5 that music is one of the most powerful tools that the Holy Spirit uses to fill us with His life-giving breath.

When most of us think about worship today, we think first about singing hymns and praise choruses. Worship involves more than singing, of course, but there are good reasons that we think of singing first. When we sing, our bodies, minds, and hearts all work together to praise God. Singing involves every part of us in a way that most spiritual practices don't. As a result, the command to sing is one of the most frequently repeated instructions in the entire Bible. Take a few minutes and read the passages below:

> *Sing to the Lord, you saints of his; praise his holy name.*

> — Psalm 30:4

> *Sing to the Lord a new song; sing to the Lord, all the earth.*
> *Sing to the Lord, praise his name; proclaim his salvation day*

after day. Declare his glory among the nations, his marvelous deeds among all peoples. For great is the Lord and most worthy of praise; he is to be feared above all gods.

— Psalm 96:1–4

Praise the Lord. How good it is to sing praises to our God, how pleasant and fitting to praise him!

— Psalm 147:1

Is any one of you in trouble? He should pray. Is anyone happy? Let him sing songs of praise.

— James 5:13

The four living creatures and the twenty-four elders fell down before the Lamb. Each one had a harp and they were holding golden bowls full of incense, which are the prayers of the saints. And they sang a new song: "You are worthy to take the scroll and to open its seals, because you were slain, and with your blood you purchased men for God from every tribe and language and people and nation. You have made them to be a kingdom and priests to serve our God, and they will reign on the earth."

— Revelation 5:8–10

Notice that singing has always been a crucial part of worshiping God. But more than that, singing is something that will *always* be a means for us to worship God. Even those who are gathered around God's throne in heaven are still singing new songs about Jesus (Revelation 5:9; 15:3), and they will continue to do so for all of eternity. If we want have a deep and life-giving relationship with God's Spirit, it's clear that singing isn't an optional activity. Singing invites the Holy Spirit to fill our hearts and change us from the inside out. Much like reading and studying God's Word, singing praise puts us in a position where the Holy Spirit can change us, moment by moment, and day by day.

> *"God himself sings over those he redeems (Zeph 3:17). He made us in his image. In some faint way, then, our singing reflects his own beauty, his generosity, his creativity."*
> — MATT MERKER[25]

Singing Transforms Us

Not long ago, our family was in a particularly difficult season of life. My father was nearing the end of his life after a long battle with cancer. Our church's financial situation was uncertain; like many churches, the Covid-19 pandemic had created challenges for us. Many people in our church community were experiencing various forms of hardship, and we didn't always have the ability to help them in a meaningful way. It was sometimes difficult to trust in God's goodness and power in our lives. Singing praise songs wasn't always at the top of my priority list. It was tough to get in the mood to sing when life seemed so hard.

One morning, though, our church's worship leader asked me to approve a new song for our weekend services. At his request, I watched a video of the group Maverick City singing the song, "Promises," which was new at the time. I remember crying as I heard the song for the first time. Take a moment and look up the lyrics online; they're powerful. The song speaks of

God's faithfulness in the midst of life's storms. It describes Jesus as an anchor, a firm foundation who will never let us down or leave us when we face trials and loss. It was the perfect song for the sadness that I was facing in those days.

As I listened, the Spirit spoke to my heart in a way that no book or sermon could have done at that moment. I was reminded of God's faithfulness throughout all of history to care for His people. I was reminded of Christ's empty tomb, which offers me a promise that my dad will one day rise again. I was reminded that God never abandons His people, even in the darkest times.

As I watched the video, I began to sing, with tears streaming down my face. I passed it along to my wife, who had the same powerful reaction. In that moment, the music transformed our hearts. Even for a few minutes, we took our eyes off our suffering and turned them toward Jesus. We were able to gain perspective, and to remember His power and His love for us.

That's what the Holy Spirit can do when we sing praises to God. He fills our lungs with His air again, giving us the strength that we need to face life's storms. That's why the Scripture commands us, over and over again, to sing praises to God. Singing helps us to personalize the truth of God's Word in a way that almost no other spiritual discipline can do. When we sing the truth, we don't just understand it, we also feel it. And when our hearts and minds are deeply connected to the truth, we are more likely to produce spiritual fruit. Singing, therefore, is a powerful and life-giving practice. So how can we build a habit of praise that permeates our daily lives?

REFLECTION QUESTIONS

- Do you have a habit of singing praises to God?
- If not, what barriers keep you from regularly worshiping Him in song?
- How can you overcome those barriers?

Bring Church Music Home

Every Sunday morning before I stand up to preach, I take my seat on the left side of our church's auditorium. From where I sit, I have a fairly good view of the people in the congregation. While I know that I ought to concentrate on singing, I sometimes find myself watching the people around me during our worship time. Don't judge me too harshly; you've probably done it too. I notice that some people are quite engaged while we're singing. They sing enthusiastically, they keep their eyes focused on the worship leader or the lyrics, and they might even raise their hands or close their eyes. However, other people seem completely disengaged. They shove their hands into their pockets, look at the floor, and refrain from singing at all. While it's impossible to tell what's going on inside somebody else's heart, I think Christians who don't engage during worship are doing themselves a disservice if they want to walk closely with Jesus.

Singing during church services isn't only beneficial while we're in the church building, though; it also helps us worship God throughout the week. The songs we sing together are meant to come home with us. If we want to build a habit of praising God on a daily basis, the best place to practice is when we gather together on Sunday morning. That's where we most often learn the songs that we can sing throughout the week, both alone and with our fellow Christians.

Think about it this way: When the Bible was written, there was no recorded music. There was no iTunes or Spotify. The only way to learn songs was if somebody else taught them to you. That learning process happened primarily in families, but it also happened when the people of God gathered together to worship Him. The nation of Israel would get together and sing from the Psalms, for example. The songs would lodge themselves in their minds, much like a catchy pop tune might get stuck in your head today. As a result, they would sing praise songs while they worked in the fields, or while they prepared their meals. Mothers might rock their children to sleep while singing their favorite Psalms. These songs were passed from generation to generation as each successive generation learned them and taught them to their children. In that way, they developed a habit of constantly singing about God's power, love, and truthfulness.

The early church continued the same pattern. There are some hints throughout the New Testament that those first Christians composed songs to help them remember what was true about Jesus. For example, many biblical scholars believe that Philippians 2:5–11 and Colossians 1:15–20 were originally hymns, written to help followers of Jesus remember what He had done for them. Whether those particular passages were hymns or not, it's clear that the early Church *did* sing hymns when they gathered, because Paul commanded it in passages like Ephesians 5:19, which we looked at earlier in this chapter. They sang praises as a group, and then they carried these songs home with them to their families and their friends.

My point is this: The easiest way to begin building a habit of praise is simply to pay attention and sing along when you're in church. As you do that, some of those songs will stick in your memory, and you'll find yourself singing them aloud during the week. If you have a hard time remembering them, ask your church's worship leader to tell you where to find recordings of the songs you sang that week, or to email you the lyrics after church. One way or another, church music is meant to come home with us.

REFLECTION QUESTIONS

- Do you pay attention during the singing times at church? If not, why not?
- How can you overcome those barriers (i.e. how can you prepare your heart and your mind to worship)?
- Do you remember the songs and carry them home with you, praising God throughout the rest of the week?

Anywhere, Anytime

A few years ago, Shannon and I were sitting in our living room when we heard the voice of our daughter singing, "Amarillo by Morning," a classic country song by George Strait. We realized that she was in the shower, singing so loudly that we could hear her from the other room. I also realized at that moment that I had a Bluetooth speaker installed in the bathroom, not far from the shower. From where I sat in the living room, then, I was able to turn on the speaker and play the same song she happened to be singing. When the music came on, we heard her suddenly stop singing, and then shout, "HEY! WHO DID THAT?" We laughed so hard we cried.

Later that evening, it occurred to me that our little moment of fun would have been impossible only a few years earlier. Never before in human history have we had the ability to listen to music so easily wherever we are, whenever we want to hear it. The ability to record and play music back is less than 150 years old. When the Bible was written, people couldn't listen to music anytime they wanted to. They only had the option of learning songs directly from people that they knew. Today we can learn new songs anywhere, at any time. Through my smartphone, I can easily find almost any recorded song in the world and play it within seconds. I can listen to my favorite music in my house, or in my car, or really anywhere at all.

My point is that it's never been easier to develop a habit of singing and listening to praise music. The hymns that I grew up singing in church, I can now stream while I get dressed for work. New praise songs are available constantly. Although it's important to exercise discernment to make sure that we're listening to songs that are consistent with Scripture, the good news is that there's a wealth of new music constantly being written, for the purpose of praising God.

In the morning while you're getting ready for your day, or while you drive to the office, or while you clean the house, you can develop a habit of praise. Turn on some praise music and – here's the important part – sing along! Don't just listen passively. Engage your mind, your heart, and your body in worshiping God.

You might object, saying, "But I have a terrible singing voice! Anybody who hears me sing is bound to become an atheist." Fair enough. Not everyone is meant to lead other people in singing. But everyone is commanded to sing to God. By way of analogy, consider the fact that not everyone is gifted to teach the Bible to other people (see James 3:1), but everyone is still commanded to read and to study the Bible anyway. Worshiping God through song is no different; it's a spiritual discipline, or breathing exercise, that God commands all of us to do. He wants us to build habits of praise, because He knows that singing His praises opens our hearts and our minds for the Holy Spirit to speak to us.

What to Sing?

Before I became a pastor, I served at a small local church for a few years as their worship leader. It was my job to select the songs to sing in each week's worship service, and to lead the congregation in praise. While I enjoyed the job for the most part, it wasn't always smooth sailing. I was hired to replace a long-time worship leader who had recently moved away. The congregation, and especially the other musicians in the worship band, had grown attached to his style over the years. That meant that they saw my style of worship as a threat. I was taking away the songs they loved and replacing them with new and unfamiliar music. Some of the members of the worship band finally asked the pastor for a meeting, to talk about me and why they didn't like my worship style. For some reason, they also invited my wife and me to attend the meeting, which meant that we had to sit quietly while several people complained about what a poor job I was doing. What I remember most vividly is when one of the singers, trying to express her disappointment with my musical selections, said, "Pastor, I'm sure some people like the songs that Matt chooses. But what about ME? What about the music I love? Where did MY songs go?"

The dilemma I experienced at that church isn't that unusual. Now that I'm a pastor, I sometimes hear the same concerns from members of my own congregation. The number of complaints doesn't necessarily depend on who's leading worship, either. If a leader sings lots of hymns, some people are unhappy. If he sings newer praise songs, different people are unhappy. If he aims for a mixture of the two, everyone is unhappy. As the old expression goes, you can't please everyone, and you'd be a fool to try.

The arguments we have over worship style often reveal something about our hearts: we're selfish and proud. We've convinced ourselves that we can only praise God if we're singing our favorite songs. The truth, though, is that God designed music as a way to focus our minds and hearts on Him rather than on ourselves. If our goal is to offer praise to God, rather than to be entertained, then we can worship Him even when we aren't singing the songs we prefer.

In Ephesians 5, Paul gives us the idea that we ought to be singing a variety of songs when we worship. He says we should sing, "psalms, hymns, and spiritual songs." While most scholars don't see a sharp distinction between these three types of songs, it does seem clear that Paul is telling us to consider different kinds of music as we praise God.

Psalms, of course, come straight from the Bible. The Psalms were written as a book of worship songs for the nation of Israel. Although we don't have any of the original tunes that accompanied the Psalms, we can still read them as a form of praise. There are also some contemporary musicians who have put the Psalms to modern music.[26]

Hymns in the ancient world were songs written to praise what was good and true about a deity. In this case, hymns are songs that contain powerful truth about God's goodness, mercy, power, and love. While hymns impact our emotions, they might have lyrics that cause us to use our minds, as well. In the English language, we normally think of hymns as having four or five stanzas, and they are a bit more formal than contemporary praise songs. They often have a four-part harmony and a fairly even and metrical rhythm.

Finally, "spiritual songs" probably refers to any song of praise to God. Spiritual songs might be less formal than hymns, with a freer lyrical structure and rhythm. Although Paul certainly wasn't thinking in terms of our modern categories of "praise song" and "hymn," it's not too much of a stretch for us to make that distinction when we think about worship music.

Whatever you think about these categories, the point is that we can worship God to almost any sort of music, ancient or contemporary, formal or informal. I would actually suggest that we should mix it up a bit and stretch ourselves. One advantage of this approach is that singing the music preferred by a different generation of Christians allows me to have deeper compassion and understanding toward them. I might also find that there are contributions that each genre of music can make to my own worship of God. Some types of songs are rich in theological truth, while others might be more emotive. Neither is bad in and of itself. We need a varied diet of praise music because God wants us to worship Him with our hearts, our bodies, and our minds.

Praise Him Anyway

Before I close this chapter, I want to make one last point about worship. As I've mentioned throughout this chapter, one reason that we sing is so that we can connect what we *believe* about Jesus with what we *feel* about Him. Singing reflects our emotions. But singing does something else: It also evokes our emotions. Sometimes we sing because we feel a certain way about God, but sometimes we sing because we *want* to feel a certain way about God. This is important.

Sometimes, when I see people singing praise songs with abandon, I think, "Wow, that person must really be feeling the goodness of God right now. She's responding to a feeling that God has been good to her, so she's singing with abandon." And quite often that's true: We sing because we are in a joyful frame of mind, so we respond accordingly.

But that's not always true. At other times, we sing aloud because we *don't* currently feel the goodness of God. But we want to, and we need to. In those moments, our songs become prayers, as well as affirmations of what is true about God. We are essentially praying, "God, this is who You say You are. Will you remind me of it, and help me to believe it? Because right now I'm not sure whether I do or not." Singing is the musical equivalent of *"I do believe. Help my unbelief"* (Mark 9:24).

Nobody is immune to feeling distant from God, separated from the life-giving breath of God's Spirit. Nobody is immune to doubt, to struggle, or to pain. When I'm struggling with those things, I don't always feel like turning on worship songs and singing along. When I hear a song about how Jesus is my living hope, or how God is a good, good Father, I might feel resistant to singing about things I'm not feeling. I am tempted to fold my arms and close my mouth.

But I've learned something important about those moments: Those are the moments when I really need to sing. So I try to sing anyway, and I sing loudly. There's often something very powerful in singing the truth about God even when I'm not feeling it. Quite often, by some miracle of God's Spirit, singing reminds me of what is true about God, and helps me to believe it again. The singing transforms my heart and my mind. Or more accurately, the Holy Spirit uses songs to transform me.

We see that pattern in the Bible, by the way. For example, we see it in Psalm 63, when a distraught and spiritually struggling man named David wrote a song to remind Himself of God's goodness. In his distress, he began to sing about and to remember who God was and what God had done. And His heart was changed, to remember and to trust God's promises.

Sometimes we sing because we feel that God is close. But sometimes we need to sing because we don't feel Him close at all. Maybe the best thing we can do to fight the darkness in our souls is to sing songs about the Light and wait for the Spirit to fill our hearts.

We've learned how to breathe the air of God's Word, and how singing praises fills our hearts with His Spirit. Next, we'll talk about prayer, as we continue our journey of learning how to breathe.

EXERCISE

Create a worship playlist composed of 10-20 psalms, hymns, and spiritual songs. Using your favorite digital music service, search for worship music and psalms there. Don't stick with only one genre of music; try to branch out a bit. If you don't know where to begin, ask your church's worship leader to help you find good praise music.

CHAPTER 6

Learning to Pray

*And pray in the Spirit on all occasions
with all kinds of prayers and requests.*

— EPHESIANS 6:18A

In the first chapter, I mentioned one of my heroes, a man named George Mueller. Mueller's work was made possible because of his rich and powerful prayer life. He was famous for spending hours in prayer each day, bringing his requests before the Lord and trusting Him to provide. Mueller's orphanage was completely dependent upon charitable gifts; he often didn't know where the money would come from to buy the food and supplies he needed to feed and house so many children. Rather than ask donors for money, though, he simply asked God to provide. On more than one occasion, God provided his orphanage with the necessary funds just in the nick of time.

For example, one morning before breakfast, Mueller was told that there was no food available for the 300 orphans they were caring for at the time. While most men would have responded with panic or despair, Mueller responded with prayer.

"God will supply," he said. He gathered the orphans together and prayed, "Dear God, we thank you for what you are going to give us to eat. Amen." At that very moment, there was a knock at the door. When Mueller opened it, the town baker was standing outside with a large tray of bread, and two additional trays in his cart outside. The baker explained that he'd been unable to sleep the previous night, because he kept thinking that the orphanage really needed that bread. Right after the baker left, the milkman showed up, offering to give them ten large cans of milk; the wheel of his cart had broken, and he needed to offload some of his milk supply before he could fix it. The milkman's misfortune and the baker's insomnia led to answered prayer for Mueller and his hungry orphans.[27]

Whenever I read stories like that, they seem distant from my own experience, though. Maybe you can relate. I know God answers my prayers, and occasionally He's done so in remarkable ways. But I lack Mueller's level of faith, and miraculous answers to prayer aren't the norm in my life. I *want* to have a prayer life like his, but I often wonder if that's even possible for somebody like me.

Even more than I want to see physical miracles, though, I'd like to experience the miracle of spiritual transformation. I long for the deeds of my flesh to be replaced by the fruit of the Spirit. The Scripture tells us that prayer can change us in profound ways. Prayer is one of the most effective ways for us to breathe the life-giving air of God's Spirit. It brings focus to our lives and teaches us to trust God more deeply. The more we pray, the more like Jesus we become.

I think most of us would agree that prayer is powerful and important. Our problem is that we don't pray nearly enough.

"The "open secret" of many "Bible believing" churches is that a vanishingly small percentage of those talking about prayer and Bible reading are actually doing what they are talking about."
— DALLAS WILLARD[28]

How Prayer is Like Flossing (But Better)

Every time I go to the dentist, I have to confront my embarrassing failure to consistently floss my teeth. I have a theory that the world is divided into two kinds of people, flossers and non-flossers. I am a non-flosser. It's not that I think that flossing is useless; I believe in flossing. I know it prevents gum disease. I've heard all the funny aphorisms that dentists like to use, like "Only floss the teeth you want to keep." Hilarious. Still, I don't actually floss much. My problem isn't a lack of good role models, either: My wife is a diligent flosser. She was born with the flossing gene, and I admire her for that.

My dental hygienist sometimes questions me about my flossing habits. I'll admit to a bit of fudging when she asks, "Have you been flossing?" I almost always *have been* flossing immediately before visiting the dentist, and I tell her so. I just don't tell her that I have *only* been flossing within the past 24 hours. But I'm not fooling her. My teeth tell their own story, silently proclaiming my failure to floss regularly.

Many of us think about prayer like we think about flossing. We know we *should* pray, and we believe that prayer makes a difference in our lives. We believe that God listens to our prayers and even that He answers them. We might have memorized passages like James 5:16, "*The prayer of a righteous man is powerful and effective,*" or 1 Thessalonians 5:17, "*Pray without ceasing.*" We've read powerful stories of men like George Mueller, who saw God do mighty things in their lives when they devoted themselves to prayer. Yet we don't actually pray much more often than we floss our teeth. When it comes to prayer, there is a huge gap between what we know we ought to do and what we actually do.

But we can't live a Spirit-filled life apart from prayer. Prayer is probably the most direct way for us to connect with God. It's also one of the most reliable ways for us to experience the power and the filling of the Holy Spirit. When we pray, the Spirit reminds us of what is true, and He corrects the lies we're tempted to believe. He changes our attitudes, making us more submissive to God's will, and He gives us power to obey God. The Bible tells us that the Holy Spirit even helps us to pray, speaking for us when we aren't sure what to say (Romans 8:26).

If prayer is really that powerful, how can we make a shift from simply believing in prayer to practicing it? How can we create consistent habits of prayer? And once we build those habits, what should we pray for?

The last thing we need is some legalistic benchmark for how often to pray, or a list of formulas to use. Instead, we simply need to put ourselves in a position where we can hear and respond to the Spirit's voice through prayer. Day in and day out, we need to plant ourselves by the living water of God's Holy Spirit. In order to do that, we need to learn how to build a consistent habit of prayer. When we do that, we'll see the Spirit transform our lives in ways that we never thought were possible.

Prayer and the Holy Spirit

Since this is a book about the Holy Spirit, we need to ask, "What does the Holy Spirit have to do with prayer?" When we pray, after all, we usually address the Father. That's appropriate, since Jesus' most famous prayer begins with the words, *"Our Father, who art in heaven"* (Matthew 6:9). And we pray in the *name* of Jesus because Jesus encouraged us to make our requests to God in His name (John 14:13–14). But we don't often think about the Holy Spirit when it comes to prayer.

But if you read the New Testament carefully, you'll see that the Holy Spirit shows up frequently when the subject of prayer is mentioned. Look at just a few of the verses that connect the Holy Spirit to prayer:

And pray in the Spirit on all occasions with all kinds of prayers and requests (Ephesians 6:18).

In the same way, the Spirit helps us in our weakness. We do not know what we ought to pray for, but the Spirit himself intercedes for us with groans that words cannot express. And he who searches our hearts knows the mind of the Spirit, because the Spirit intercedes for the saints in accordance with God's will (Romans 8:26–27).

I urge you, brothers, by our Lord Jesus Christ and by the love of the Spirit, to join me in my struggle by praying to God for me (Romans 15:30).

But you, dear friends, build yourselves up in your most holy faith and pray in the Holy Spirit. Keep yourselves in God's love as you wait for the mercy of our Lord Jesus Christ to bring you to eternal life (Jude 20–21).

> *Pray without ceasing; in everything give thanks; for this is God's will for you in Christ Jesus. Do not quench the Spirit (1 Thessalonians 5:17–19, NASB).*

Over and over again, the Scripture tells us that we approach God through the power of His Spirit, and the Spirit is the one who teaches us to pray. The Spirit also listens to our prayers and speaks to God on our behalf. He is deeply involved in our prayer lives.

But why does the Holy Spirit care so much about our prayers? He cares because prayer is one of the primary ways we can connect with Him. And the more we connect with the Spirit through prayer, the more effectively He can transform us into the image of Jesus.

"To pray is to change. Prayer is the central avenue God uses to transform us."
— RICHARD FOSTER[29]

Prayer Changes Us

Many years ago, a college student approached me after church on Sunday and said he had a question to ask me. I could tell he was feeling a bit embarrassed about it, and I assumed he was going to ask me about some private sin struggle, or maybe ask my advice about a recent breakup. Instead, he took a deep breath, looked me in the eye, and said, "Do you think it's a sin for me to pray that God will give me a pretty wife?"

I had to pause and consider his question carefully. There's nothing in the Scripture that forbids a young man from praying for a pretty wife, so I couldn't exactly tell him it was a sin.

On the other hand, I felt confident that he could pray for much greater things than that. God created beauty, of course, and He also created marriage. Wanting an attractive spouse isn't a bad desire. It's just not the primary concern we should have when we pray. Our primary concern in prayer is to become more like Jesus. As we talked, this student began to see that a better prayer would be to ask God to make him a godly man. That would be a worthwhile prayer, whether he ever got married or not. And if he ever *did* get married, he would be much better equipped to love his wife well, whatever she happened to look like. He would be much more likely to have a marriage – and a life – that honored Jesus.

My conversation with that student illustrates a common temptation we all face when it comes to prayer: We pray for what we want instead of what God says we need. As a result, we feel disappointed when He doesn't answer our self-centered prayers.

The Scripture never says that God will give us everything we want. It *does* promise that He will hear our prayers and they will transform our hearts. For that reason, prayer is critical for every Christian who wants to produce the fruit of the Spirit. When we pray, we are actively breathing Spirit-filled air, and that air changes us profoundly. When we pray, God's Spirit rubs off our rough edges and makes us more like Jesus.

Let me offer a couple of biblical examples of how the Spirit uses prayer to change our hearts. In Philippians 4:6–7, Paul wrote, *"Do not be anxious about anything, but in everything, by prayer and petition, with thanksgiving, present your requests to God. And the peace of God, which transcends all understanding, will guard your hearts and your minds in Christ Jesus."* Notice that Paul didn't say, "Present your requests to God, and He will give you everything you want." Instead, he said that when we present our requests to God, He will give us His peace. Peace, of course, is listed among the fruit of the Spirit in Galatians 5. When we pray, we put ourselves in a position where the Spirit's peace can fill our hearts. We are breathing the air of the Spirit's peace, and that air transforms us.

We see that same principle in the book of James. James tells us that if we need wisdom, we should simply ask God to give it to us (James 1:5). Wisdom, of course, is the ability to make God-honoring decisions amidst the challenges and concerns of our daily lives. James 3:17–18 (NASB) says that the wisdom that God provides produces spiritual fruit in our lives:

> *But the wisdom from above is first pure, then peaceable, gentle, reasonable, full of mercy and good fruits, unwavering, without hypocrisy. And the seed whose fruit is righteousness is sown in peace by those who make peace.*

Do you notice the overlap between the character qualities James lists here, and the fruit of the Spirit in Galatians 5? James is saying that when we're full of God's wisdom, we'll produce the fruit of the Spirit. How can we be full of God's wisdom? We can pray. When we pray for wisdom, God makes us wise. He aligns our thoughts and our desires with His perfect will. Prayer, then, is an exercise in submitting our lives to the transforming power of God's spiritual wisdom.

When we pray, we must ask ourselves, "Am I seeking my own will for my life or God's will?" We're often puzzled when God doesn't answer our prayers in the ways we want him to. All too often, that's because we are not submitting our desires to His will. We're praying for what we want, instead of what God knows we need.

However, God always answers us when we pray, "Lord, make me more like Jesus." When we ask Him to transform us into the image of Jesus, God always says, "Yes." Before we pray that God will change the world, we need to pray that God will change our hearts.

How do we develop prayer lives that lead to that sort of spiritual transformation? Let me suggest three practices to help you create a consistent prayer habit: Find the right time, find the right place, and remove the distractions.

"Increasingly, time pressures crowd out the leisurely pace that prayer seems to require . . . Where does God fit into a life that already seems behind schedule?"
— PHILIP YANCEY[30]

Find the Right Time

When I was a college student, I found that I was different from many of my friends in one significant way: I liked to go to bed early. I never pulled an all-nighter during college, not even to study for a test the next day. I believe in the law of diminishing returns; after midnight, there really isn't any point in studying anymore, at least not for me. I won't remember anything I've studied the next day. To this day, my own children tease me for going to bed around 9:30 P.M. I am simply not a night person.

On the other hand, getting up early in the morning has never been much of a problem for me. I don't enjoy getting up at 5:00 A.M., but I can if it's necessary. Most days I get up around 6:00. That's the best time for me to pray. The house is quiet, and I normally have about an hour before everyone else begins to stir.

Everyone is different, though. Maybe your best time for prayer is during lunch, or at night after everyone else has gone to sleep, or in the car during your morning commute. The Bible never says that one time of day is more spiritual than another time of day. Psalm 88:1 says, *"O Lord, God of my salvation, I cry out day and night before you."* The Psalmist apparently prayed whenever he could, whether that was in the morning or at night. The prophet Daniel made it a habit to pray three times a day, morning, noon, and night (Daniel 6:10). Whenever you can pray, that's the right time to pray.

Consistency is critical, though. Whenever you pray, do so regularly. You probably eat your meals around the same time each day. If you exercise, you probably do so at the same time every day. Developing a habit of prayer requires that same sort of consistency. It will probably take two or three months of praying at the same time each day before it becomes a deeply ingrained habit in your life. Pick a time that works and stick to it tenaciously.

Don't be overly ambitious, though. If you're not used to praying regularly, an hour will feel like an eternity. And if prayer feels too burdensome, you're likely to give up. Instead, carve out 15 minutes, and slowly increase your time allotment from there. As you become more and more proficient in prayer, you'll find that 15 minutes is no longer enough.

You might also find that the best time of day changes as you enter different stages of life. The key is to keep praying, even when your schedule changes. If one time of day no longer works, find a new time that does. As we saw in our chapter about engaging with God's Word, we make time for the things that matter to us. If it's important to us to pray, then we'll carve out time to pray.

Let me offer one more thought on the subject of when to pray: Some people will say that we don't need a set time for prayer, but instead that we ought to pray throughout the day as we go about our normal lives. To some extent, I agree. 1 Thessalonians 5:17 tells us to pray without ceasing; we can and should pray constantly. However, something powerful happens in our minds and our hearts when we set aside a specific time of the day to pray, when we aren't focused on anything else. It's during those moments that we can hear the Spirit's voice most clearly and respond to Him, without the distractions that often cloud our minds when we're engaged in our everyday routines. For that reason, it's a good idea to set aside a special time every day to focus on prayer alone.

EXERCISE

Look at your calendar right now. Find one or two times when you can consistently spend 15 minutes in prayer each day. Make an appointment for prayer in your calendar. If somebody asks you to schedule something else during that time, you can simply say, "I already have something planned."

Find the Right Place

When my wife Shannon and I were in our first year of marriage, we visited my grandparents' house at Christmas time. I was only one of their nine grandchildren, and all of us were visiting at the same time. My parents, brothers, aunts and uncles, and a number of other family members were also there, which meant that the house was overflowing with people. One afternoon, Shannon and I wanted to have a private conversation, but we quickly realized that there was nowhere to go where we could be alone. So we went outside and sat in our car. However, one of my uncles found us about three minutes later and asked me to roll down the window so he could chat with us. We finally gave up and just went back inside.

The dilemma Shannon and I faced is the same one that many of us face when we try to pray. It can seem nearly impossible to find a quiet and private place to talk to God. I live in a home with four other people and a dog. If I go into the living room early in the morning, I'm certain to wake up the dog, who is often sleeping nearby. If the dog wakes up, then the kids will wake up, and my prayer time is effectively over. On the other hand, if I try to pray aloud while lying in my bed, I might disturb my wife.

I've resolved this problem by praying in our bedroom closet. I can slip out of bed and close the closet door, where I'm able to pray without waking anybody up. That works for me. I've known some people who go outside and sit on the back porch where they can be alone. Others have an office or a quiet room where they can go. When my kids were very young, I would often slip out of the house early in the morning and go for a long prayer walk. My point is that if you want to pray consistently, it helps to find a place where you will not be disturbed.

You might be thinking, "That sounds great if you have enough space, but I live in close quarters with a large family. There's not a private place anywhere." Or maybe you live in a small dorm room with another roommate. Let me encourage you with the story of Susanna Wesley. Susanna had ten children, two of whom were John and Charles, the future founders of the Methodist Church. Susanna lived in a very small home with many young children, and her husband was often away traveling. She was a godly woman who believed in the power of prayer, but she didn't have a private place where she could talk with God. Instead, when it was time to pray, Susanna Wesley grabbed her apron and threw it over her head. She would pray in her little makeshift apron-tent, while her children played and did schoolwork all around her. It wasn't ideal, but it worked for her.[31]

My point is that if prayer is important to us, we will not only find the time, we can also find a place. Building a prayer habit requires diligence, perseverance, and just a little bit of creativity.

EXERCISE

Walk through your home and find a good place to pray. Where will it be quiet at the time you've chosen for prayer? Where can you be undisturbed, away from your electronics or other distractions? In the space below, write down which room or area you've chosen.

Remove the Distractions

"It takes time to quiet your mind and your heart before the Lord . . . It is a spiritual discipline to be still, to listen, and to cut out the distraction and din of our world. And as we practice this stillness, this waiting,

It's no secret that most of us feel addicted to our smartphones. I recently ran across some statistics about cell phone usage that are rather shocking. For example, the average American spends 5.4 hours each day on their phone. Over the course of forty years that amounts to about *nine years* spent looking at a phone. 66% of the population demonstrates signs of something called "nomophobia," which is the fear of being without your phone.[33] As a result, we bring our phones everywhere. We sleep next to them, we carry them into the bathroom with us (might as well admit it), and we allow them to interrupt our conversations and daily tasks. I'll admit that I'm guilty, as well; I hate seeing my "screen time" report pop up every week. I'm often ashamed of how many hours I spend looking at the screen.

Smartphones aren't all bad, of course. They allow us to communicate with one another in ways that were previously impossible. There's no question, though, that it's hard to pray – or to practice any spiritual habit – when your phone is next to you, alerting you of every email, text message, Facebook comment, and news story. Sustained concentration is a dying art, and that has potentially grave consequences for our ability to know God deeply.

When it comes to prayer, then, we need to separate ourselves from all kinds of distractions, but especially from our phones. It isn't easy, but it also isn't impossible. I'm often tempted to bring my phone into the closet with me when I pray. I convince myself that I need it to know what time it is, or just in case I need to look up a Bible verse. Those are excuses, though. I have a watch.

I have physical copies of Bible. I don't need the phone with me while I pray.

Try leaving your phone in the other room for thirty minutes while you pray. Shut it off or set it to "do not disturb." It's extremely unlikely that anything critical will happen on your phone while you're praying. And it's easy enough to check it again when you're finished praying.

Disconnecting from distractions helps us create the quiet environment that we need in order to hear the Spirit's voice. I've found that the Holy Spirit doesn't like to shout over the noise of my daily life. He *can* shout, but He prefers to whisper. If we are always surrounded by noise, it's harder for us to hear Him speaking.

Years ago, a friend of mine suffered a back injury that required him to lie still for hours at a time. He wasn't able to hold a book or even to look at his phone. Even watching movies on his iPad became too difficult. He was forced to just lie there, with nothing to distract him from his own thoughts and feelings. He later told me that, as painful as it was, that was one of the most spiritually transformative times of his life. Almost as soon as he was forced to be quiet, he heard the Spirit's voice say to him, "Are you ready to listen to me now?" And he was. After all, he had nothing to distract him. That's the power of finding consistent quiet time to be still in God's presence. When the Spirit is ready to speak, we'll be ready to listen.

Once we find the right time and place, and we remove unnecessary distractions, we're ready to pray. But it might surprise you to learn that prayer begins not with talking, but with listening.

Listen Before Speaking

Dare I admit that listening is hard for me? My wife tells me that I don't always listen to her very well. I've had to work on that throughout our marriage. It isn't that I don't care about what she's saying; I care about it a great deal. It's just that listening is hard. Sometimes when she starts talking, I think about how I plan to respond. Or maybe I think I have the solution to her problems. Or that I know the perfect words to put what she's saying in its proper perspective. Or, even worse, there might be some other topic that I want to discuss, and I'm waiting for my turn to speak. Listening requires patience and selflessness.

When it comes to prayer, listening is probably even *more* difficult, because the Spirit rarely speaks audibly, and He doesn't always speak right away. We have to be patient and allow for silence. We have to shut off our instinct to immediately tell God what we think or what we want Him to do. It can be hard to pause and listen for His voice.

Listening to God is a learned art. It might help you to read a short section of Scripture first, to prime your heart and mind to hear from God. After reading it, pray something along these lines, "God, I am here to hear from You. I'm listening for Your voice and asking you to speak." Then simply sit quietly and wait for a few minutes. Before you begin offering God your own thoughts, feelings, and desires, make it a habit to listen to Him.

The reason for listening is simply this: Our primary goal as we pray is to align our will with God's will. The Scripture provides us with much of what we need to know about God's will, which is why we need to read it constantly. But the Spirit of God also speaks to us when we are quiet, and He helps us apply God's Word to the circumstances of our daily lives. Listening to God is a powerful form of breathing Spirit-filled air.

If you've never practiced this sort of spiritual listening, you will wonder at first how you can know when God is speaking to you. That's a great question, and there is no simple answer to it. It is kind of like asking somebody, "How will I know when I'm in love?" When God's Spirit is speaking, He will always say things that align with His Word, of course. He will never tell you to cheat on your spouse, or to steal from your employer. Beyond that, I've found that His voice often provides specific peace, wisdom, and comfort for the daily situations I face. Rarely – if ever – do I get specific information about the future, or about what I should do today. And as I mentioned, His voice isn't audible most of the time. Instead, the Spirit's voice sounds more like the quiet assurance that He is in control. It sounds like the *"peace that passes understanding,"* that Paul described in Philippians 4. It sounds like the "wisdom that comes from above," gently guiding me to the thoughts and attitudes that He wants me to have (James 3:17–18).

Just like any relationship, the more we practice listening, the more we will recognize the Spirit's voice. If He doesn't seem to be speaking to you at the moment, don't worry. Just keep practicing. Once you've allowed some time for the Spirit to speak, it's time to consider what to say.

> *"Learning to pray, like learning to talk, read, or walk, takes time and involves trial and error. The process will doubtless include feelings of awkwardness and failure."*
> — PHILIP YANCEY[35]

Learning the Language of Prayer

When our daughter was a toddler, she had a unique way of speaking that very few people could understand. For one thing, she used the word "pa" and "ma" to refer to a host of different words. "Pa" could mean "pass," "pray," "peas," "pear," or something else entirely. "Ma" could mean "more," "mine," "my," or "meat," just to name a few. She would string together long sentences that consisted of nothing other than those two words. "Pa ma ma pa pa," meant, "Pass me more peas please." As her parents, we grew accustomed to her way of speaking, so we could understand her about 75% of the time. Almost nobody else could, though. Over time, however, she slowly learned how to speak in a way that everyone could understand. I'm proud to say that today, she speaks nearly flawless English (she's 17 as I'm writing this). She just needed to learn our language, and learning a language takes a lot of practice.

In the same way, it takes a lot of practice to learn the language of prayer. It doesn't come naturally to most of us. For one thing, we are finite, sinful people trying to speak to an infinite and holy God. For another thing, we can't see God, and we rarely hear His voice speaking audibly. It takes practice to know what to say to an invisible God.

The good news is that Jesus gave us a model for how to pray. You've probably read the Lord's Prayer before; maybe you grew up reciting it in church. It's recorded in Matthew 6:9–13, right in the middle of Jesus' Sermon on the Mount. Before reciting the prayer, Jesus provided a couple of important prayer principles for His listeners.

First, He said that prayer isn't a performance. We don't pray to impress other people. Instead, prayer is communication. We're talking to God. Second, Jesus told His followers not to babble. Certain pagan religions taught that the gods would listen to you more attentively if you repeated the same mantras over and over again. Some Eastern religions still practice this. But Jesus told His listeners that all they needed to do was to talk to God like they would speak to another person. He then provided them with a model of what a good prayer ought to look like. That's what we call The Lord's Prayer.

What's important to understand about the Lord's Prayer is that Jesus didn't intend for us to merely repeat it. There's nothing wrong with reciting it, of course; I've memorized it, and I meditate on it often. But our prayers weren't meant to begin and end with recitation. Instead, Jesus was giving us a simple pattern to follow, in order to demonstrate the sort of things we ought to pray about. Think of the Lord's Prayer like a template; it provides us with a structure to use as we're building the content of our own prayers. If we want to know what to pray about, the Lord's Prayer gives us just a little bit of direction. With that understanding, let's look at the elements of the Lord's Prayer and how we can incorporate them into our own prayer lives.

Praise, "Hallowed Be Your Name"

The Lord's Prayer begins with the words, *"Our Father, who art in heaven, hallowed be your name."* Or at least that's how it is phrased in the King James Version of the Bible. As a kid, I always wondered what "hallowed" meant (and also, I wondered, who was Art?). In case you still wonder, "hallowed" means, "regarded as holy or sacred." It is an old-fashioned way of saying, "God I pray that your name will be honored and revered." Jesus is encouraging us to pray that God will be respected and revered for who He is, the perfect and righteous King of the Universe.

When we pray that God will be honored, we're acknowledging that He is worthy of all the honor in the universe. In essence, then, the Lord's Prayer begins with praise. Praise is a great way to begin our own prayers, as well. Before we ask God to meet our needs, we should take a moment to acknowledge who we're speaking with. God is holy, all-powerful, perfectly loving, infinitely gracious, and so much more. Praise helps us remember that He is God and we are human.

Here's a helpful prayer exercise: Make a list of reasons God is worthy of praise. For example, He is merciful, He knows everything, He is the source of all good gifts, and so on. If you need help, read the Psalms. Or read J.I. Packer's excellent book *Knowing God.* The second section of Packer's book provides some great information about God's character and attributes. Once we know more about who God is, we know better how to praise Him. Keep your list beside you as you pray. Perhaps you can focus on one praiseworthy attribute each day. For example, praise Him for some specific ways in which He's shown His love to you and to the world. Once you've spent the first few minutes praising God, it's time to intentionally align your heart with God's will.

EXERCISE

Take a few minutes right now and begin your list of God's praiseworthy attributes. Next to each one, jot down one or two Bible verses to help you remember them. Here are just a few to get you started:

- God is love (1 John 4:8). We know this because He sent His Son Jesus (1 John 4:9; John 3:16).
- God is sovereign (Jeremiah 32:7; Proverbs 19:21; Psalm 115:3). We know God is sovereign because He made the universe (Colossians 1:16–17).
- God is wise (Romans 11:33). We know He is wise because He gave us His perfect Word (Psalm 19:7–11).

Continue the list on your own, with attributes like holiness, grace, and others.

Submission: "Your Kingdom Come"

Every four years, it feels the United States loses its collective mind as we prepare for another presidential election. In recent years, the anger and division surrounding politics in our country has only gotten worse. We've moved far beyond simple disagreements about which candidate or party is best to lead our country. The prevailing mindset seems to be that anybody who disagrees with us isn't merely wrong, but also evil. Politics has become a sharp line, dividing our country into many competing factions. Each faction feels they're on the side of righteousness and truth, arrayed against the forces of evil and darkness represented by the opposing political party. Each side has a different vision of what a perfect nation should look like. We argue loudly over which kingdom is best, the kingdom on the right or the kingdom on the left?

Jesus tells us that there is a kingdom of righteousness that stands opposed to the forces of darkness and evil in the world. It isn't a kingdom aligned with the rulers or political parties of this nation, though. It's the kingdom of God. Jesus wants to make us faithful citizens of His kingdom, so much more than He wants us to be loyal members of our political parties.

The second part of the Lord's Prayer addresses this allegiance to God's kingdom: "*Your kingdom come, Your will be done, on earth as it is in heaven.*" Jesus told us to pray that God will realign our hearts, so that our first allegiance is to His kingdom. He commanded us to pray that God will reshape our desires to be in conformity with His will.

That's a painful and difficult prayer, because it requires our personal desires to give way to God's will. We can easily convince ourselves that we're praying for God's will to be done, when in fact we're praying that the rest of the world would conform to *our* will. We feel that God's kingdom should align with our values and preferences, rather than the other way around. We want God to build His kingdom with the materials that we select: our opinions, our political beliefs, our favorite people, and so on. The Lord's Prayer is calling us to do something entirely different, which is to conform our beliefs, convictions, and preferences to those of King Jesus.

Whenever we pray the Lord's Prayer, we are praying that Jesus will bring His kingdom to earth quickly. But we're also praying that He will make us into people who reflect His kingdom values right now. We're asking Him to implant the values of His kingdom into our hearts, to turn us into kingdom representatives who share His priorities and values.

When we pray, then, we must ask God to show us the misplaced allegiances and upside-down value systems that are preventing us from reflecting His kingdom. We must come before Him with open hands and open hearts. We pray for His kingdom to come, not only through Christ's return, but also through the renovation of our faithless hearts.

When we begin to pray this way, the Holy Spirit will change us. This sort of prayer waters the roots our lives, producing in us the fruit of the Spirit. Only once our hearts are aligned with God's will are we then prepared to bring Him our requests.

REFLECTION QUESTIONS

1. Are you tempted to believe that your personal opinions and value systems are always the same as God's?
2. Are you willing for Him to change your perspectives through His Word and His Spirit? If so, do the exercise below.

EXERCISE

Pray something like this, "God, I want to be like Jesus. Before I ask for anything from you, I want to be aligned with you. Show me where I've tried to create Your kingdom by trusting in the kingdoms of the world. Help me see where my values and priorities don't align with Your will but are instead my own preferences and priorities. Change me into a faithful and submissive kingdom representative today."

Petition: "Give Us This Day Our Daily Bread"

Jesus' prayer continues with the words, *"Give us this day our daily bread."* He moves from submission to petition. However, the request Jesus offers is very specific and very limited in its scope. He doesn't say, "God, please provide enough money for the next year." He doesn't really pray for anything remarkable. Instead, Jesus just says, "God, please give us enough bread for today."

Keep in mind that in Jesus' day, people didn't take it for granted that they would have enough food to eat each day. Without modern technology – things like refrigerators and complex preservatives – most people had to prepare or purchase food on a daily basis. Every morning, they had to trust that God would provide food and water for that one day.

I don't think that Jesus was trying to say that we ought *only* to pray for small, everyday needs, though. Instead, Jesus wanted us to understand how desperately we need to rely upon God in every moment. We are dependent upon Him just to remain alive. God is the Source of all life, and He is the Sustainer of all life. As we said in Chapter 3, without the Spirit's breath in our lungs, we would quite literally die.

There are a variety of prayers in the Bible. Some are simple, like this prayer for daily bread. Others are more complex, like Paul's prayer for spiritual growth for the Colossian believers (Colossians 1:9–12). But every prayer in Scripture highlights our complete dependence upon God. Everything happens because God either causes it to happen or allows it to happen. Therefore, when we pray for His provision, we acknowledge that He is in control of our lives and in control of the universe. The Lord's Prayer reminds us that even having enough food to eat is a matter of God's grace.

It's in that spirit, then, that we offer our petitions to God. We can't demand His compliance. Instead, we come before Him like subjects before our King, with humility and open hands. Even Jesus, facing death on the cross, petitioned God with an attitude of humility and surrender: *"Going a little farther, he fell with his face to the ground and prayed, 'My Father, if it is possible, may this cup be taken from me. Yet not as I will, but as you will'"* (Matthew 26:39). He trusted His Father completely, even though He still had to go to the cross. In the long run, of course, God saved humanity through His obedience, and Jesus was exalted above every other name in the universe (Philippians 2:5–11). Therefore, the Father did something much greater than saving Jesus from the pain of death. Jesus prayed with an attitude of complete surrender, trusting His Father's perfect plan. The Lord's Prayer calls us to pray with that same attitude of submission.

How do we know what to pray for, though? Fortunately, the Holy Spirit is ready to help.

---

*"Imagine a loving parent seeking to help a child . . .
As the youngster struggles to express his feelings and
desires, the parent imparts knowledge, and with his own
lips, carefully tries to formulate what the child wants to
say. This is a picture of how the Holy Spirit catches up
our deepest longings and aspirations and brings them
in line with the Father's ultimate purposes for us."*
— THOMAS CONSTABLE[36]

The Spirit Helps Us

Every year around November, my family starts asking me what I want for Christmas. It's always a little bit stressful to me if I'm honest. When I was a kid, I had no problem rattling off dozens of gifts that I thought would make me happy. As an adult, things are a bit more complicated. The material items I want are much too expensive for my family to buy; I can't very well ask for a Porsche. And much of what I want can't be bought. I want my family and friends to be healthy and happy. I want my kids to grow up wise and successful. I want freedom from the insecurities and sin struggles that haunt me. None of that can be wrapped up and placed under the tree. It's hard to know what to ask for.

Often when we pray, it's similarly hard to know what to ask for. Sometimes we have deep desires that we can't express in words. Other times, we're not quite sure what would be the best request to make in a particular situation. What can we do, then? How can we decide what to pray for? As I mentioned earlier in this chapter, the Bible promises us that the Holy Spirit will speak to God on our behalf. Romans 8:26 says, *"In the same way the Spirit also helps our weakness. We do not know what we ought to pray for, but the Spirit Himself intercedes for us with groans that words cannot express."* When we don't know what to say, the Spirit fills in the gaps for us. That should provide reassurance if you're feeling stressed about your prayer life.

We can also read the Bible if we want to get better at praying according to God's will. The Bible gives us many ways in which we can pray for ourselves, our communities, and our world. Here is a partial list:

- Pray for spiritual growth, for ourselves and for others (Jude 20; Colossians 1:9–12; Ephesians 1:15–19).
- Pray for the gospel to be proclaimed and believed (2 Thessalonians 3:1–2).
- Pray for physical needs and provision (Matthew 6:11; 3 John 1:2).
- Pray for physical healing (James 5:13–16).
- Pray for those in positions of authority (1 Timothy 2:1–4).
- Pray for personal requests and desires (1 Samuel 1:10–20; Philippians 4:6).
- Pray for wisdom to make God-honoring decisions (James 1:5).
- Pray for comfort for those who are grieving or suffering (2 Thessalonians 2:16–17).

This isn't an exhaustive list, but it's enough to get us started. If we consistently prayed for these requests, for ourselves and our loved ones, we would have powerful prayer lives.

One way to help focus our prayers is to make a prayer chart using the biblical categories above. I've included an example in Appendix 3. For my own prayer chart, I start by making a column for each day of the week, Sunday through Saturday. Then I divide my chart into different groups of people, with one row for each group. There's a row for myself, another row for my family, another for my Christian friends, another for non-Christian friends, and so on. Every day, I lift up different requests for each group of people, using the list above. For example, on Monday I might pray for my children to grow spiritually and to make wise decisions at school. On Tuesday I might pray for them to boldly share the gospel with their non-Christian friends, and so on throughout the week. As their circumstances change, or when my prayers are answered, I adjust the chart accordingly. This method helps me to remain focused and specific when I pray.

When God answers my prayers, I try to write that down somewhere. Many years ago, my wife and I created a poster that we kept behind the door of our bedroom, where we wrote down some ways God had answered our prayers through the years. Consider doing the same thing. If not a poster, perhaps you can keep a list of answered prayers in your phone somewhere or write it down at the bottom of your prayer chart. Wherever you record them, make a point of remembering how God has been faithful to your prayers. Remembrance is especially helpful in those moments when prayer seems futile, or when we have doubts about God's goodness.

Just as we said about reading the Bible, an effective and transformative prayer life is a matter of showing up, day in and day out, to connect with the Holy Spirit. As much as we would like a shortcut or a simple formula, there isn't one. Great men and women of prayer know that consistency is the most important quality to have if we want to walk closely with the Spirit. He transforms our hearts slowly, one day at a time, as we submit our hearts to His will, and present our requests before Him.

EXERCISE

Using the example in Appendix 3, create a prayer chart of your own. Use it as a guide to offer your own requests before the Lord. Try this method for about a month, and then adjust your chart if necessary.

What About Unanswered Prayers?

When I read about prayer warriors like George Mueller, I feel inspired, but I also feel confused sometimes. Why did he experience such immediate and dramatic answers to his prayers, while my own prayers often go unanswered? What did Mueller do right that I am doing wrong?

First, it's important to realize that not all of Mueller's prayers were answered immediately or affirmatively. Those stories aren't always the ones that get told. For example, George Mueller was widowed twice, although he prayed fervently for both of his wives to be rescued from death. Even the most faithful prayer warriors have no guarantees that God will answer their every prayer with a "yes." Jesus Himself prayed that God would spare Him from crucifixion, but He also submitted Himself to the Father's will and went to the cross for our sake (Matthew 26:39). We aren't necessarily praying wrongly when God doesn't grant every request.

Second, I have to admit that I don't pray as often or as faithfully as Mueller. I've come to believe that people like George Mueller experience greater power in their prayer life simply because they pray more frequently. Prayer truly was like breathing for George Mueller; it occupied a large portion of his day. He believed firmly that God would answer him. When he didn't receive what he asked for, he simply trusted God's will and kept on praying. He never let bitterness or unbelief to stop him from prayer. Over time, as his own will was conformed to God's will, he began to see the Lord answer his prayers in astounding and dramatic ways. In other words, it's not that Mueller was somehow better than you and me. It's just that he was better-practiced in the art of prayer.

Finally, there are some circumstances that can hinder our prayers. Sometimes it's just that God's timing is different from ours. Sometimes He has His own mysterious reasons for doing what He does. And sometimes our own sinful actions and attitudes prevent Him from answering us. In Isaiah 1:15, God told the Israelites that He wouldn't listen to their prayers as long as they were oppressing the poor and the vulnerable among them. Similarly, 1 Peter 3:7 warns husbands that treating our wives unkindly can result in unanswered prayer. That's why the final portion of the Lord's Prayer provides us with a model for dealing with sin in our lives. Sin blocks our prayers, but confession clears the air.

Confession and Cleansing: "Forgive us our trespasses"

The Lord's Prayer ends with these words, "*Forgive us our debts, as we also have forgiven our debtors. And lead us not into temptation, but deliver us from the evil one*" (Matthew 6:12–13).[37] The "debts" Jesus refers to here are not financial, but moral. When we sin against God or against others, we are falling short of our obligations to them. We deserve punishment, and that debt must be paid.

Sin is the biggest barrier we face in breathing Spirit-filled air. It separates us from God and prevents us from hearing His voice. Because of its importance, we are going to dedicate the following chapter to the concept of confession and cleansing. Dealing with sin is a critical skill for the spiritual life, so we want to consider it carefully and thoroughly.

Before we move to that topic, however, I want to offer one final exhortation: If we want to cultivate a life-giving relationship with the Holy Spirit, we must learn to pray. We must build time into our lives on a regular basis, and we must learn the language of prayer. We'll need to set aside some of the ways we typically spend our time and energy. We'll need to submit our will to God's will, even when it's painful. However, the benefit is worth the pain. We believe that *"the effective prayer of a righteous person accomplishes much"* (James 5:16). Learning to pray isn't an easy road, but it's a journey worth taking.

REFLECTION QUESTIONS

1. After reading this chapter, what is one area of your prayer life in which you'd like to grow?
2. What is your biggest challenge related to prayer, and how can you begin to overcome it?

CHAPTER 7

Spiritual Purification

*When I kept silent, my bones wasted away
through my groaning all day long. For day
and night your hand was heavy upon me;
my strength was sapped as in the heat of
summer. Then I acknowledged my sin to
you and did not cover up my iniquity. I said,
"I will confess my transgressions to the
Lord"— and you forgave the guilt of my sin.*

— PSALM 32:3–5

When I was a kid, my mom gave my brothers and me a Flintstones vitamin pill every morning before school. I suppose she wanted to supplement our diet with some extra nutrition. Perhaps she hoped the vitamins would make us taller; if so, it didn't work. Despite the fact that the vitamins resembled characters from a popular cartoon, they didn't really taste very good. Perhaps they taste better these days, but back then none of us liked taking them. We took them anyway, though, because Mom told us to.

Or at least I *thought* we all took them. One morning while I was brushing my teeth, I suddenly became curious about a broken drawer in our bathroom vanity. Ever since I could remember, the drawer had been stuck closed. There was a very small space between the front of the drawer and the cabinet, but this drawer was effectively unusable. But that morning, for some reason, I decided to force it open. I grabbed the drawer with both hands and pulled as hard as I could. When it opened, I saw that this broken bathroom drawer was full of Flintstones vitamin pills. Since my younger brother David shared the bathroom with me, I knew immediately how the pills got there. For years, he had been dropping his morning vitamin pills into that small gap, assuming that nobody would ever open the drawer and see what was inside. I still don't understand why David didn't simply bury the pills at the bottom of the trash can. I guess he figured as long as the pills were out of sight, he would never get caught.

My brother's approach to those vitamins is the way many of us deal with sin in our lives. We try to hide it and to keep it out of view. We're afraid that if anybody else finds out about our sin, they'll reject us, and sometimes we're right about that. Acknowledging our sin also forces us to admit that we aren't as righteous as we like to think we are, and that reality threatens our self-image. We are forced to face the fact that we've become trapped in cycles of sin that we can't escape, no matter how hard we try.

If we are going to live a Spirit-filled life, though, we must bring our sin into the light and deal with it. Sin is like bad air; it poisons our lives and threatens to choke out our ability to connect with God. We can't breathe the pure air of God's Spirit when we're trying to hide from His conviction and transformation. For that reason, the Lord's Prayer ends on a note of confession. *"Forgive us our trespasses as we forgive those who trespass against us,"* Jesus prayed. *"And lead us not into temptation but deliver us from evil"* (Matthew 6:12–13). Jesus knew confessing our sin leads us to spiritual healing and growth. Confession opens up our spiritual lungs so that we can breathe God's purifying air.

"He who confesses and condemns his sins already acts with God. God condemns thy sins: if thou also dost condemn them, thou art linked on to God."
— ST. AUGUSTINE[38]

A Stealthy Killer

Not long ago, our daughter began to urge us to install a carbon monoxide detector in our house. A safety expert had visited her school and warned the students of the dangers of carbon monoxide poisoning. Carbon monoxide is a byproduct produced by burning natural gas, oil, coal, or other fuels. It can emanate from your gas oven, your car, or even your dryer. Breathing it into your lungs will kill you. The problem is that carbon monoxide is invisible, tasteless, and odorless. As a result, it can kill you before you even know that anything is wrong. A carbon monoxide detector sounds an alarm, warning you of the presence of the deadly gas. That's your signal to leave your home and call 911.

Sin works in much the same way as carbon dioxide. It fills our spiritual lungs with poisonous air. It can creep up on us and ruin us before we even recognize that we have a serious problem. James 1:15 tells us that *"when sin is full-grown, it leads to death."* Sin separates us from God's life-giving presence and wreaks havoc on our spiritual lives. To avoid sin's devastation, we must be vigilant not only to recognize it, but also to confess it and eliminate it from our lives. We must be ruthless with our sin; it isn't something to trifle with.

The Holy Spirit is like a spiritual carbon monoxide detector. He convicts us of our sin and urges us to alter our course. We need the Spirit desperately, because sin is often subtle and hard to recognize. Sometimes we're aware of the "big" sins in our lives, since those are tough to ignore. When we explode with anger or look at pornography, for example, we usually feel guilty. But "smaller" sins are easily overlooked. Sins like pride, envy, and bitterness can take root in our hearts slowly and quietly, doing a great deal of damage before we notice they're even present.

In Jesus' Sermon on the Mount, He talked about how murder springs from hateful thoughts, and adultery springs from lust (Matthew 5:21–30). We think of murder and adultery as major sins, and most of us try to avoid them. The same was true in Jesus' day; most people figured that as long as they weren't doing the really terrible stuff, they were spiritually healthy. Jesus corrected that short-sighted understanding of sin. Walking with God isn't simply a matter of avoiding the really ugly and visible sins. Instead, we want to reflect God's character with our thoughts, attitudes, and actions. To accomplish that, we need the Spirit to transform us from the inside out. Sin always grows in our hearts and our minds before it spreads to our hands and feet. Nobody goes to jail just for hating somebody. But hatred leads to violence if it's allowed to grow unchecked. We might not think that lust is all that bad, as long as we don't act on it, but lust inevitably lead to sexual immorality when it's allowed to run rampant in our minds.

If attitudes like love, joy, peace, and patience are the fruit of God's Spirit, attitudes like hate, discontent, and lust are the spiritual weeds that threaten to choke that fruit. Weeds are deadly, but they're also sneaky. I almost never notice weeds in my yard while they're growing. I only notice them once they're threatening to choke out my grass. As a result, I try to be proactive. I take early preventive measures to keep the weeds from popping up, like fertilizing the grass and applying weed killer. Keeping the weeds at bay requires constant vigilance. Sin is the same way.

When we remain connected to the Spirit's voice through the Scripture and through prayer, we are taking proactive steps to root sin out of our lives. We won't achieve perfection until we meet Jesus face to face, of course. But through prayer and confession, we can prevent sin from taking over our hearts and rupturing our fellowship with God. Sin grows quickly in dark and hidden places, but confession brings it into the light where God can root it out of our lives. Confession is a spiritual weed-killer.

Like any other spiritual practice, however, confession requires discipline. Moment by moment, day by day, we need to take constant inventory of our hearts and confess our sin as soon as we are aware of it. Of course, confession also requires a painful degree of humility. Admitting our sin shatters our illusions of self-righteousness, forcing us to acknowledge how deeply we need God's transforming power.

"Confession begins in sorrow, but it ends in joy.
There is celebration in the forgiveness of sins
because it results in a genuinely changed life."
— RICHARD FOSTER[39]

The Consequences of Spiritual Pride

When my kids were young, one of their favorite Shel Silverstein poems was called, "Sarah Cynthia Sylvia Stout Would Not Take the Garbage Out." If you've never read it, the story is more or less revealed by the poem's title. For some reason, probably mere obstinance, Sarah Cynthia Sylvia Stout simply refused to take out the trash. She did other chores around the house, like cooking or washing the dishes, but she let the garbage pile up. Little by little, garbage filled up her home, eventually pushing through the roof and piling up to the sky. Sarah's friends no longer came over to play, and the neighbors all moved away because of the smell. By the time she finally relented and tried to deal with the trash, it was too late. Garbage had covered the entire country, apparently swallowing Sarah herself. The poem ends by telling us that Sarah suffered an awful fate, one too terrible to mention.

I always think of that poem when I think of the consequences of unconfessed sin. Sin starts small, much like Sarah Stout's pile of garbage. An angry thought here, a discontented attitude there, and before we know it, our lives are overrun with sin and we're out of control. The real danger we face is becoming too proud and stubborn to confess our sin. Just like Sarah, when we pretend our sin doesn't exist, we only make it worse. Sin doesn't simply disappear on its own; instead, it grows worse and worse, threatening to destroy us in the process. 1 John 1:6–10 (NASB) addresses the peril of refusing to acknowledge our sin:

> *If we say that we have fellowship with Him and yet walk in the darkness, we lie and do not practice the truth; but if we walk in the Light as He Himself is in the Light, we have*

fellowship with one another, and the blood of Jesus His Son cleanses us from all sin. If we say that we have no sin, we are deceiving ourselves and the truth is not in us. If we confess our sins, He is faithful and righteous to forgive us our sins and to cleanse us from all unrighteousness. If we say that we have not sinned, we make Him a liar and His word is not in us.

Few of us have a hard time seeing other people's sins, but we struggle to recognize our own. This struggle isn't an observational problem, but a spiritual one. We are *intentionally* blind to our own disobedience. We know that acknowledging our sin will require us to make some painful and difficult changes to root it out. But as long as we can deny or excuse our wrongdoing, we never feel the need to change. We fear the hard work of pulling the spiritual weeds from our hearts.

John understood this tendency, which is why he warned us against the attitude that says, "I have no sin to confess." We are all tempted to lie, when the alternative is to face up to the darkest parts of our hearts. We lie not only to God, but to other people, as well. And we even lie to ourselves. We rationalize our sins by saying that they probably aren't as bad as someone else's. "Sure, my mind and heart are full of garbage, but other people are worse," we tell ourselves. But we're fooling ourselves; sin damages us profoundly, no matter how small it seems.

When we lie about our sin, we're deliberately hiding from God's presence. We are actively preventing the Spirit's breath from filling our lungs. As a result, we damage our relationship with God and we compromise our ability to represent Jesus effectively to the world around us.

We need to understand that God already knows everything we've done wrong. Despite our best efforts, we can't hide from him. And the longer we try, the worse things will get. The Bible is filled with stories of men and women who tried to hide their sin from God, but instead reaped terrible consequences. Adam and Eve. Achan. King Saul. Ananias and Sapphira. The list goes on and on.

God's Word offers us good news, though: When we confess our sin, God is eager to forgive. He delights in cleansing our hearts and filling us up with His Spirit. For that reason, confession should be a regular practice. We need to begin by taking an honest inventory of our spiritual condition.

REFLECTION QUESTIONS

- What are the recurring sins that you are tempted to deny or hide?
- Do you rationalize your sin by saying that it's not that bad, or that somebody else's is much worse?
- If somebody points out an area of sin in your life, are you humble or are you defensive? Why?

Taking Inventory

Several years ago, our family's home flooded in the middle of the night. A pipe burst while we were sleeping, covering the floors with dirty water from underneath the house. The damage was extensive, requiring us to move out of our house for several weeks while it was being repaired. The first step was for an insurance adjuster to come over and assess the damage. I watched him as he walked from room to room with a clipboard, writing down everything he saw that needed repair. Then, the insurance company asked us to take inventory of any personal items that were destroyed by the water: books, electronic devices, clothing, and more. To restore our lives to normal, we had to take a full inventory of everything that was damaged. It would have been counter-productive for us to hide or minimize the damage, since our goal was to make our lives whole again.

That same principle applies to our relationship with God. If we hope to get our spiritual house in order, we must begin by taking an honest inventory of what's broken inside of us, at least as well as we can. Where have we fallen short of God's design for our lives? In what ways have we refused to submit to His will, believing that we know better? We have to be as specific and detailed as we possibly can.

We struggle with specificity, though. When I was a kid, I knew that confession was supposed to be a part of my prayer life, so I prayed something like this: "God, please forgive me for all the sins I committed today." That prayer made me feel like I'd confessed my sin, but I actually hadn't confessed anything at all. That approach wouldn't fly in our human relationships, of course. If you call your spouse a terrible name in the heat of an argument, they won't be impressed with an apology that goes like this: "Mistakes were made, and I regret all of them." In order to reconcile the relationship, you have to be specific; you have to confess exactly what you did wrong. The same thing is true when we confess our sins to God. Admitting that you're a sinner in general is different from confessing specific transgressions against God.

Nehemiah 1 provides an example of what it looks like to confess specific sins to the Lord. Nehemiah was written around 445 B.C., just over 100 years after the Jewish people were exiled to Babylon because of their idolatry. King Cyrus of Persia had allowed them to return to Jerusalem, but the walls of the city remained broken down, and the people still languished in poverty. When Nehemiah, who was still living in Babylon, heard the news, he sat down and wept for days on end. He realized that his countrymen were experiencing God's discipline because of their sin. They were suffering because they were still in rebellion against God. As a representative of the nation, Nehemiah confessed their sins to the Lord, and asked for His forgiveness.

His prayer is refreshingly honest and specific. He admits that God's people have rebelled against Him, refusing to obey the law of Moses. He acknowledges that they have been "unfaithful," a word that quite often refers to idolatry (1:8). Nehemiah is painfully honest, admitting that even his own family had been complicit in disobeying God (1:7). He doesn't hold anything back or try to protect his own reputation. He takes an honest and complete inventory of the sins that the people had committed, including his own.

We can learn from Nehemiah's example as we take inventory of our spiritual lives. Confession requires honesty and courage. It requires taking constant inventory of the ways in which our attitudes, words, and actions don't line up with God's Word. Where have we failed to exhibit the fruit of the Spirit? Remember all of the reflection questions in Chapter 3 about the fruit of the Spirit? Those questions are one way to take an inventory of your heart. You can return to them on a daily basis to discern where your life doesn't match up with Christ's character.

Our goal is to keep short accounts before God. Confession isn't something we do once every six months, or even once a week. We must constantly evaluate our lives and confess our sin as soon as we're aware of it. Take a few moments now and work through the evaluation exercise below.

EXERCISE

Pause now and spend a few minutes taking inventory of your life:

- In the past 24 hours, where have your thoughts and attitudes failed to reflect the fruit of the Spirit? For example, have your thoughts been judgmental, lustful, or selfish?
- Have you spoken in ways that don't reflect the character of Jesus? For example, have you said things that were unkind, untrue, or crass? Have you failed to encourage someone, or to speak the truth when it was called for?
- Have you used your body – your hands and feet, your eyes, your sexuality – in ways that are contrary to God's Word?

Spend a few moments confessing your sins to the Lord and asking for His forgiveness. Be as specific and thorough as possible.

Truly Clean

"When you sin, do a thorough job of repenting. Re-hate sin all over again. Consecrate yourself afresh to the Holy Spirit and his pure ways. But reject the devil's whisper

With a family of five, it seems like our dishwasher is constantly running. I don't understand how we use so many dishes in a single day. The sink fills up with dishes, so we load the dishwasher and run it. By the time the dishes are clean again, the sink is filled with a new pile of dishes. And on and on it goes. The biggest challenge for us is that we aren't always sure whether or not the dishes in the dishwasher are clean. I know there are magnets you can buy that say "Clean," on one side and "Dirty," on the other, but we've never gotten around to buying one. We open the dishwasher at least once a day and ask, "Are these clean? I can't tell." It's important to know if a plate or a bowl is clean before you eat from it, but the evidence is not always clear.

On the other hand, Christians who confess their sin to God can know for sure that they're clean. 1 John 1:9 says that when we confess our sins, God cleanses us from *all* unrighteousness. We don't have to wonder if we've really been forgiven. We don't have to worry that God might be holding a grudge. He is infinitely gracious and eager to restore us to close fellowship with Him again.

For the Christian who has trusted in Jesus, of course, we never need to worry that our sin will permanently separate us from God. Romans 8:16 says, "*The Spirit Himself testifies with our spirit that we are children of God.*" Once you've trusted in Jesus, the Holy Spirit constantly reminds you that you are God's adopted son or daughter. For that reason, Romans 8:38–39 tells us that "*nothing can separate us from the love of God which is in Christ Jesus.*" Once a child of God, always a child of God.

When we sin, though, we interrupt our fellowship with Him. That's why we confess our sin; it restores our closeness with God. We don't confess our sin to make sure we're still saved. Our relationship with God is permanent. That's why the Scripture describes us as God's children, not as His employees or acquaintances. I have three children, and sometimes they disobey me. Their disobedience strains our relationship, but it doesn't sever it. Parents don't fire our own children as if they're employees. Instead, we work through their disobedience in order to restore our sense of closeness. Quite often, they need to acknowledge their disobedience and ask for forgiveness. And confession goes both ways in human relationships, of course; sometimes parents have to confess and apologize to their children, too. Confession clears the bad air and restores trust and intimacy. Of course, God never needs to confess sin, since He is morally perfect. We must confess our sin regularly, though, to restore our close fellowship with Him.

John says that when we do confess our sin to God, He is quick to forgive. Then we can know for certain that we're clean. If you're like me, you're probably tempted to wallow in shame even after you've confessed your sins to the Lord. Not only is that unnecessary, it's harmful. When I refuse to believe that I'm forgiven, I only increase the distance between God and me. As a result, I'm likely to drift even further into sin. "After all," I reason, "if I can't draw near to God again, why even *try* to obey Him?" That's why Satan tries to accuse us and shame us even after we confess. Accusing God's people of sin is one of the primary strategies Satan uses to keep us from breathing the air of God's Spirit.[41] Our enemy wants us to believe that God couldn't possibly love us anymore, so we have no choice but to keep our distance from Him.

But nothing could be further from the truth. Ever since He first revealed Himself to the nation of Israel, God has declared Himself to be *"compassionate and gracious, slow to anger, and abounding in lovingkindness and truth"* (Exodus 34:6). When Jesus arrived on the scene, God's grace and compassion became even clearer (John 1:16–17). The Holy Spirit makes it clear that not only is God willing and eager to forgive us, but also that He wants to live inside of us permanently, even though we still struggle with sin. We can let go of the shame that keeps us from intimacy with God, knowing that the Spirit has washed us clean.

In His kindness, God also gives us a number of tools to help us in our fight against sin. The Holy Spirit's conviction leads us to confession, and His power transforms our character. But He also provides us with another resource to help us in our struggle against temptation: the community of faith.

Confessing to Other People

One of the most remarkable spiritual revivals in American history occurred in 1970 at Asbury College, a small Wesleyan school in Wilmore, Kentucky. On February 3, the dean of the college was scheduled to preach a sermon at chapel. Instead, he shared a short personal testimony of how God had been working in his life. Then he invited students and faculty to share their own stories. Before long, students were lined up to share what God was doing in their lives.

That unusual chapel service became a powerful movement of God's Spirit when students began to step forward and confess their sins in front of their classmates and professors. Nobody coerced them to confess or manipulated them into sharing their darkest secrets. Instead, the students themselves somehow understood that public confession would lead them to deeper relationships with God and with one another. Remarkably, that chapel service extended for nearly eight days, at which point classes were finally resumed. Across the United States, college students were inspired by the Asbury Revival, and similar movements sprang up across the country.[42]

At the heart of almost every extraordinary movement of the Spirit is the practice of confession. More specifically, spiritual renewal often begins when people not only confess their sins to the Lord, but also to their fellow Christians. Confessing our sins to one another often forces us to bravely confront it and to take steps to eradicate it. In addition, when others are aware of the sins we struggle with, they can pray for us and hold us accountable.

Throughout the Bible, when the Spirit was about to do something new and powerful, He often led God's people to confess their sins to one another. When Jesus was beginning His public ministry, people came to the Jordan River, both to confess their sins and to be baptized by John. When Paul began to preach the gospel and perform miracles in Ephesus, those who believed in Jesus confessed their sins publicly (Acts 19:18). The apostle James told first-century Christians that physical healing was possible when Christians gathered together, prayed, and confessed their sins to one another (James 5:14–16). That sort of confession paves the way for the Spirit of God to cleanse our hearts and prepare us for God to work. Confession expels the bad spiritual air and makes room for the life-giving oxygen of the Holy Spirit.

Many years ago, I was meeting with two pastor friends of mine for prayer. We had been meeting regularly for a few months, mostly to share prayer requests and spend some time getting to know each other. One afternoon, one of the other men asked us if he could share some personal sin struggles that he was facing. He was specific and honest in his confession, and he was clearly repentant. He wanted to change, and he knew that he needed prayer and accountability in order to do so. I could tell that he was also embarrassed and fearful, though: What if we rejected him? What if we were horrified and repulsed by his confession?

Instead of isolating us from one another, though, his confession drew us closer together. We prayed for him, but we also began to confess our own sins. Together, the three of us prayed for God's forgiveness and for the strength to resist temptation. That little gathering became a routine part of my schedule for the next decade, and it was a spiritual lifeline for all three of us.

Confessing my sin and praying with those two men transformed my life. I still struggle with sin, of course, but confessing my sin to trusted friends makes those battles less intense. I feel less afraid of temptation, and less ashamed of failure, because I know that other men who love me unconditionally are praying for me. The Spirit of God has used that time of confession to draw me closer to Jesus and to conform me further into His image.

What about you? Are you hiding your sin, trying to conquer it all by yourself? Is there anybody in your life who knows your deepest struggles and sins? You don't have to stand on a stage and share your deepest secrets with hundreds of other people. In fact, that isn't usually the appropriate way to approach confession. But the Bible does tell us to confess our sins to *somebody* else so that they can pray for us.

I encourage you to seek out one or two close Christian friends with whom you can confess your sin and ask for prayer. Maybe you're isolated from Christian community right now; if that's the case, pray and think about how you can reconnect. Maybe you can join a Bible study or a prayer group. Or perhaps you can call your pastor or spiritual mentor and ask for prayer.

Confession involves risk, of course, so we must be discerning and cautious. Look for people who are trustworthy, and whose lives are marked by the grace of Christ. Spend some time together before you dive into deep personal issues. But don't give up on seeking friends who can help you draw closer to Jesus. Don't let shame or fear of rejection keep you from community.

Community is critical in every aspect of our spiritual lives, of course, not only for confessing sin. That's what we'll discuss in the next chapter. Up to this point, we have focused on how we can breathe the air of God's Spirit in our personal lives. But we also need to talk about how to breathe His air in unison with other followers of Jesus. How can we find a good community of believers, and how can we engage with that community in way that will draw us closer to Christ?

REFLECTION QUESTIONS

1. Is there anybody in your life you trust enough to share your struggles and sins with? Can you ask somebody to pray for you on a regular basis to have the strength to resist temptation?

2. If you feel alone in your struggles, ask God to provide a friend or two who can walk beside you as you endeavor to walk more closely with the Spirit.

CHAPTER 8

Breathing Together

For we were all baptized by one Spirit into one body—whether Jews or Greeks, slave or free— and we were all given the one Spirit to drink.

— 1 CORINTHIANS 12:13

When my wife Shannon and I were in our 20s, we moved to Dallas. I took a position as the worship leader at a relatively small church. Wanting to connect with people quickly, we decided to join a small group Bible study through the church. But we had a hard time finding information about how to sign up. The church didn't have a website (yes, it was a long time ago), and we didn't see any information about Bible studies in the church bulletin. One Sunday morning we decided to simply ask some people sitting near us how to sign up. What happened next is still burned painfully into my memory. Shannon approached a middle-aged couple and asked them, "Can you tell us how to join a Bible study?" The other woman shrugged her shoulders and said, "I don't know. But our group is full."

Looking back, I don't think she was trying to be rude or intentionally exclusive. In her mind, she was just stating the facts – she couldn't help us, and there wasn't any room left in her group. But her response put us on guard. Would we be accepted at this church? Or were they closed off and unwilling to welcome new people? If I hadn't been on staff, we might not have returned for a second visit.

Now that I'm a pastor, I often remember that moment when I see guests walk into our church. I assume that some of them have been hurt at church before; many of us have. Church should be a place where people are welcomed warmly and loved unconditionally. Sadly, it's not always like that. Churches are full of all kinds of people. Some are walking with the Spirit closely, and they fill the air around them with His joy and life. Others are selfish and immature and draining spiritual oxygen from the room. Church can be a place of deep healing and spiritual growth, or it can be a place of terrible pain and frustration.

If you've been hurt by the church, you're probably tempted to give up on it. You might find it hard to believe that God wants the church to be a place where His Spirit is present and powerful. The church is one of the primary tools that God wants to use to transform us into the image of Jesus though. If you're tempted to give up on church, I'd like to encourage you in this chapter to give it another try. And if you do belong to a church, I want to call you to faithfully engage with God's people there. The Scripture tells us that the Holy Spirit does some of His most awe-inspiring work when Christians breathe His life-giving air *together*. Something special happens when we not only walk with Jesus as individuals, but also as a community. As imperfect as it is, the church is a miracle of God's grace and power.

REFLECTION QUESTIONS

- How do you feel about church right now? Do you see it as a gift from God to help you to become more like Jesus? Or do you see church as a place where you have experienced more pain than healing?
- If church has been a place of pain for you, what would it take for you to give it another chance?

United by the Spirit

If you're old enough (and I am), you might remember a movie from the 1980s called *The Breakfast Club*. If you haven't seen it, I don't recommend that you go watch it; it's not particularly wholesome. The movie was quite popular in its time, though, and it's become a bit of a cult classic in the years since it was released. The story centers on a group of five high school students who are confined one Saturday to an all-day detention: a popular girl, a brainy nerd, a jock, a troublemaker, and one girl who is shy and bit strange. The students are not friends when the day begins; in fact, they'd rather not be in the same room together. Over the course of the day, though, they come to understand each other in deeper ways. They find that they have a lot more in common than they imagined. By the end of the day, they learn to respect and even to like one another.

The message of the film, of course, is that even people who are different from us might turn out to be good friends. The movie resonated with lonely teenagers, because adolescents long for a place to fit in, somewhere they'll be accepted just as they are. In real life, it's hard to find a place like that, where people of different interests, abilities, and backgrounds can all come together and get along. *The Breakfast Club* wasn't exactly realistic, of course. It's extremely rare to see such a diverse group of people getting along with one other, especially in high school. Our world tends to divide people up on the basis of economic class, physical appearance, race, political affiliation, nationality, gender, and a host of other traits. Just scroll through social media and you'll see how divided our world truly is.

The beauty of the church, though, is that it isn't held together by earthly character traits. It's held together by the power of the Holy Spirit. Whenever we gather, the Spirit is present and active among us. He binds His people together and fills us with deep love and a unity that can only come from God. Unlike any other organization on the planet, the church is a place where the Holy Spirit fills the atmosphere. Below are a few passages from the Bible that connect the church to the power of the Holy Spirit:

> *When the day of Pentecost came, they were all together in one place. Suddenly a sound like the blowing of a violent wind came from heaven and filled the whole house where they were sitting. They saw what seemed to be tongues of fire that separated and came to rest on each of them. All of them were filled with the Holy Spirit and began to speak in other tongues as the Spirit enabled them.*
>
> — Acts 2:1–4

*For we were all baptized by one Spirit into one body—
whether Jews or Greeks, slave or free—and we were all given
the one Spirit to drink.*

— 1 Corinthians 12:13

*There is one body and one Spirit, just as also you were called
in one hope of your calling; one Lord, one faith, one baptism,
one God and Father of all, who is over all and through all
and in all.*

— Ephesians 4:4–6 (NASB)

*In him the whole building is joined together and rises to
become a holy temple in the Lord. And in him you too are
being built together to become a dwelling in which God lives
by his Spirit.*

— Ephesians 2:21–22

Notice the theme of unity that flows through all of these passages. In 1 Corinthians 12, Paul says that the Spirit unites people across different races and economic classes. In Acts 2, people from different countries, many of whom spoke different languages, were suddenly and dramatically united by the Holy Spirit; in fact, they were miraculously able to communicate with one another. Continuing with the unity idea, Ephesians 4 uses the word "one" seven times, and the word "all" three times. Paul's point is that *one* Spirit unites *all* Christians in the church in *one* faith.

If you know Jesus Christ, you are united together with everyone else who knows Him, no matter where they're from or what language they speak. And the identifying mark of a Christian is the Holy Spirit! It's not our ethnicity, race, economic background, gender, or political affiliation. God designed the church to be a place where everyone is welcomed on equal terms; only the Holy Spirit makes that possible.

That's why racism, classism, ageism, and other forms of discrimination have no place in the church. It's not because of a political position that we aim for unity across earthly boundaries. Instead, we seek unity because the Spirit of God is building an entirely new community, one where earthly distinctions can't keep us from worshiping Jesus together.

Of course, the church isn't always unified in reality. Because of our sin, and our failure to consistently walk in the Spirit, we don't always respond to people in ways that are consistent with God's values. Jesus gave His life to bring men and women from every tribe, tongue, people, and nation into His kingdom (Revelation 5:9–10). He sent the Spirit to make us into *"a chosen people, a royal priesthood, a holy nation, God's special possession"* (1 Peter 2:9). Yet sometimes Christians forget that when we exclude people from the church based on earthly categories like race, class, gender, nationality, or occupation, we're denying the power of God's Spirit to unite His church. If you have ever experienced that sort of exclusion or dismissal in church, I am deeply sorry; that's not how things are supposed to be. My prayer is that you won't give up, though, until you find a church that exemplifies the unity of the Holy Spirit.

"People are hungry for human experiences and the church is perfectly positioned to offer exactly that. In fact, the church is fundamentally designed and intended for this work – to create spaces and opportunities

*for people from all walks of life to experience true
human flourishing, in real time and real space."*
— JAY KIM[43]

Growing Together

When I was in college, I dreaded group projects. The problem is that each individual member of the group has very little control over the outcome. I tend to be a highly driven individual; I like to finish projects early, and I like them to be done well. In most groups, though, there's at least one person who doesn't care whether the work is done on time or done well. Other group members have to pick up the slack, and they usually resent it. It's frustrating when people don't do their part. Groups are supposed to work together to accomplish their goals. Everyone should contribute, bringing his or her own strengths, knowledge, and best efforts to the table.

Whether we like it or not, spiritual growth is a group project. Nobody does it alone. Throughout this book, we've discussed how to put ourselves in a position where the Spirit of God can change us, moment by moment, and day by day. Mostly, we've looked at ways to do that as individuals. But the Spirit also changes us through our relationships with other Spirit-filled people. The Spirit speaks to us powerfully through the community of faith.

That's why the writer of Hebrews commanded, *"Let us consider how we may spur one another on toward love and good deeds. Let us not give up meeting together, as some are in the habit of doing, but let us encourage one another—and all the more as you see the Day approaching"* (Hebrews 10:24–25). When we worship and serve God together, we have a transformative impact on one another's lives. We help one other produce the fruit of the Spirit and avoid the deeds of the flesh. We encourage each another to walk more closely with the Spirit as we all seek to become more like Jesus.

I'm going to make a statement that will probably sound extreme to some people, but I believe it's true: There is no way to become spiritually mature if you're completely disconnected from the church. The church is the only organization that Jesus Himself promised to build and to protect (Matthew 16:18). The church is also the only organization where the Holy Spirit lives. He lives inside every Christian, of course, but He also lives in all of us together. When the church meets, the Spirit moves and speaks to us in ways that He doesn't when we're all by ourselves. We need the body of Christ, the church, if we want to be like Jesus.

I realize, of course, that there are some people who cannot physically attend church. Some people have illnesses or other limitations that prevent them from going to church on a weekly basis. If that is your situation, God knows, and He is gracious. You aren't sinning if you *can't* go to church. I believe that part of the responsibility of the local church is to connect with and care for those who can't go to church through no fault of their own. For example, our own church has made a practice of visiting local nursing homes to lead worship for the residents and to connect with older men and women who are unable to get to church each week.

On the other hand, there are some Christians who *choose* not to connect with the body of Christ through a local church. Perhaps they've been hurt in the past; perhaps they simply prefer to stay home and rest on Sunday. If that describes you, the Scripture is clear that you are short-changing your own spiritual development and withholding your spiritual gifts from the rest of God's people. If we intentionally isolate ourselves from the body of Christ, we will find ourselves short of spiritual breath. When we gather, though, the Spirit uses the church and its people to transform us into Christ's image.

How the Church Transforms Us

Several months ago, I was eating at a local Mexican restaurant with a co-worker of mine. I love Mexican food, especially tortilla chips, taco shells, and shredded cheese. As I mentioned in the first chapter, my cholesterol is sometimes a bit high, and my love of tortilla chips is one reason for that. Anyway, I was standing in line to order, right behind my co-worker, and an internal battle was raging in my mind. I knew that I should probably order a salad. I had recently been to the doctor for my annual exam, and he'd gently encouraged me (i.e. threatened me) to take it easy on the carbs. But a salad didn't sound good to me that day. I wanted a giant burrito, one the size of my head.

As I stood in line deciding what to do, I heard my co-worker ordering his meal. He ordered a salad. That surprised me, because he loves chips, queso, and salsa at least as much as I do. I realized at that moment that if he could resist temptation, then so could I. I reluctantly followed suit and ordered a salad too. Notice that my co-worker didn't have to nag me to eat something healthy. He didn't even tell me why he chose a salad that day; he wasn't even aware of my internal dilemma. It's just that his wise choice convicted me to make my own wise choice.

That story highlights one of the ways in which spiritual transformation happens in the body of Christ. We don't go to church primarily to hear good sermons, although sermons can help us understand the Bible and apply it to our lives. But we're often impacted more by the people sitting next to us than by the person standing onstage.

For example, I know some people at my church who are exceedingly generous. They freely share their homes, their cars, their money, and whatever else they have, with those in need. When I see people like that, the Spirit convicts me to consider how I use my own resources. I know other Christians who are much more joyful than I am. As I observe that particular fruit of the Spirit in their lives, I'm convicted to pray for greater joy and contentment in my own life. I find myself asking God to transform me, because I've seen others in my church modeling the fruit of the Spirit in ways that I don't.

My close friends at church don't simply *model* Christ-like character, though. They also lovingly point out areas where I need to grow. They live the truth, but they also tell me the truth. We all need people to hold us accountable, to challenge us to become more like Jesus. We also need encouragers, people who remind us to stand firm in our faith when we feel like giving up. Finding those people is one reason it's so important to connect with a church.

The Bible assumes that spiritual growth happens in the context of community. The Scripture never endorses the idea that my spiritual life should consist of God and me alone, with no encouragement or accountability from my fellow Christians. God's Word assumes – and commands, in fact – that we seek growth in the context of a local church.

The writer of Hebrews warns us that neglecting to meet together actually puts us in danger of forsaking the faith completely. But when we do gather together, we are able to *"spur one another on toward love and good deeds."* The phrase "love and good deeds" appears to be a concise way of describing the fruit of the Spirit. In addition, the Greek word translated as "encourage" in verse 25 is a form of the same Greek word used in John 14:16 when Jesus refers to the Holy Spirit as our "Helper." I don't know if that connection was intentional, but the writer of Hebrews seems to be saying, "People who are filled with the Helper need to *help* each other produce the fruit of the Spirit." For that reason, planting ourselves in a position where the Spirit can transform us means planting ourselves within a community of faith.

REFLECTION QUESTIONS

- What do you look for in a church? What do you try to avoid?
- Can you think of a time in your life when you grew spiritually as a result of being connected to the body of Christ? Why did you grow in that particular church?

How to Find Your Community

I still vividly remember the night before I started 7th grade. I was awake in my bed until almost 3:00 A.M., tossing, turning, and fretting. I was anxious about finding my place in the harsh social landscape of junior high school. My biggest concern was this: Where would I find friends? Who would be my people? Nothing is more important to a teenager than finding somewhere to fit in.

We never really outgrow the desire to fit in, though. Sadly, some of us have struggled in the past to find our fit within the church. Churches can be complicated sometimes but finding the right one isn't impossible. If the Holy Spirit lives in you, I believe He wants to help you find the right place, a place where you can build deep relationships to help you follow Jesus. Here are a few practical questions to ask as you search for a church home:

- *What does this church believe?* Most churches have some kind of statement of beliefs posted on their website. It probably explains what they believe about Jesus, the gospel, the nature of God, and other critical issues. Consider whether the church holds to traditional Christian doctrines, like the humanity and deity of Jesus, the Trinity, salvation by grace through faith alone, and the truthfulness of the Bible.[44]
- *What is this church's mission?* Every church is called to the same basic mission, to make disciples (Matthew 28:18–20). To put it in simple terms, a disciple is a follower of Jesus. When you investigate a church, then, ask if the church focuses on sharing the gospel and helping Christians know Jesus better. If a church is inwardly focused, pouring all of its energy into keeping its current members comfortable and happy, it will eventually decline and die. Find a place that is spiritually vibrant, equipping its people to be evangelists and disciple-makers.
- *How does this church worship?* I'm not talking about whether the worship band sings hymns or choruses. Instead, it's important to ask if church services follow the patterns we see described in the New Testament. Is

there sound teaching from God's Word? Does the church observe communion on a regular basis? Are new believers baptized as a public demonstration of their faith in Jesus? These basic functions characterize a church with healthy patterns of worship.

- *How are decisions made at this church?* Not every healthy church uses the same type of leadership structure. Some churches give more authority to the congregation, while others have a board of elders that makes most of the decisions. However if all the decision-making power belongs to one person, that's a red flag. If one pastor has unilateral authority to make all of the decisions, with no accountability, I suggest going elsewhere. In a healthy community, decisions are made transparently, and multiple voices are allowed to speak into the process. Ask a few current members if they trust and respect the leadership at the church.

- *Are there opportunities to build deep relationships at this church?* Ask some of the church's members if it's easy to connect with their community. Is there a clear and simple pathway for you to find a group of Christians who can help you grow? You'll still need to take some initiative, of course. No church can make friends for you if you don't put in any effort. But a healthy church will offer clear-cut ways for you to begin building relationships.

- *Are there opportunities for you to serve?* We'll talk more about this in the next chapter, but we all have spiritual gifts and abilities designed to build up the body of Christ. We attend church in order to grow closer to Jesus, but also to help other people grow closer to Him, as well. One of the ways we help is by serving wherever the church needs us. Seek out a church where you can participate in meaningful ways. If all of the ministry is performed by paid staff, keep looking around until you find a church where everyone can be involved in service.

- *Are people at this church actively seeking to become like Jesus?* As we've discussed, one of the main benefits of the church is that it helps us to walk more closely with the Spirit. We need our fellow Christians to help us produce the fruit of the Spirit. As you interact with the people at your church, then, consider whether you see the Spirit at work in their lives. Every church will have its struggles and its sins but look for signs of growth and spiritual fruit. Are members of this church gracious, truthful, and Christ-like? Are they seeking to become more like Jesus on a daily basis? If so, then it's likely to be a healthy church.

When it comes to finding a church, by the way, I am *not* advocating that you look for a perfect place without any conflicts or disagreements. As the old saying goes, "If you find a perfect church, don't join it; you'll only ruin it." Conflict is inevitable whenever two or more people are gathered together. In fact, conflict is usually a necessary ingredient for us to grow. God uses people with different viewpoints and struggles to sharpen us. In the same way that healthy conflict can strengthen a marriage, the *right* kind of conflict can strengthen a church as well. What matters most is whether the church approaches conflict with the grace and truth that comes from knowing Jesus. Our goal is to find a healthy church, not a perfect church.

"It's easy to fake the fruit of the Spirit among people we pick as fellowship partners. It's far

more difficult to pretend love, joy, peace, patience, kindness, goodness, faithfulness, gentleness, and self-control among those who irritate us."
— MICHAEL SVIGEL[45]

How to Connect

Perhaps you've found a healthy church community to join, or you already belong to one, but you're not sure exactly where to start making connections. Here are a few ideas to help you take the first few steps:

- *Show up.* It should go without saying that you can't build deep relationships with people you never see. That's true in marriage, in parenting, in friendships, and in the church. If you want to connect with other Christians, you have to go to church regularly. We don't go to church to check it off a list, or because we think Jesus will like us more when we're at church. We attend church because we need to be around God's people. Proximity leads to transformation.

- *Initiate relationships.* Whenever somebody tells me that they can't find any friends at their church, I always ask if they've initiated with anyone. Sometimes people come to church, sit at the back of the room, and wait for others to befriend them. As a pastor, I certainly encourage our staff and leaders to look for new people and reach out to them, because we really want people to feel welcome. Relationships aren't one-sided, though; making friends requires a little bit of initiative. Say hello to people, invite them to spend time with you, and communicate that you're interested in building connections. It takes time to build relationships, but the outcome is worth the effort.

- *Join a small group.* Most churches have Bible studies or home groups where you can not only learn about the Scripture, but you can also connect with people. Like any spiritual discipline, connecting with other Christians will require setting aside some time. Aim to carve out some time to meet during the week with a group of other Christians for prayer, Bible study, and encouragement. If your church doesn't offer groups at times when you can meet, ask somebody in leadership if you can start your own. Many pastors will welcome that offer and will give you their blessing.

- *Don't give up too easily.* This last point might be the most important one. If you've found a church that preaches God's Word, offers a place for you to connect, and appears to be healthy, don't leave simply because it takes a while to build relationships. The most meaningful relationships I have in my life were not built over a period of a few months, but over the course of many years. If you think about it, the same is probably true in your own life. Maybe you belong to a church, but you feel out of touch with it. Don't give up quite yet. Perhaps you simply need to invest a bit more prayer, time, and effort into finding the connections you're longing for.

The Reward is Worth the Risk

Throughout my years as a college pastor, I often spoke with college men who were trying to decide whether or not to ask a girl out. Sometimes their hesitation had nothing to do with the girl herself; they were just terrified of rejection. There was always a chance that the girl they were interested in would turn them down. And everyone knows that rejection hurts. On the other hand, though, these men wanted to get married one day. And the harsh reality is that there is no way to begin a relationship without a certain degree of risk. That's the way life goes, and that's not only true in the arena of dating. Every human relationship involves risk.

Relationships within the church are no exception to that rule. Building life-transforming relationships with other Christians is risky. Some people might reject you or exclude you. They might hurt you, intentionally or accidentally. If you connect with other people, you'll eventually get hurt.

But relationships can also provide us with life-changing love and spiritual transformation. I've been hurt at church, but I've also been healed. I've been cut down, but I've also been built up. I've seen other Christians manifest the deeds of the flesh, but I've also seen beautiful displays of the fruit of the Spirit. On balance, the reward of pursuing Christian community has been worth the risks I've had to take. The Spirit speaks to me through my fellow Christians in ways that He doesn't speak to me when I'm all alone.

The beauty of the church is that God's people can breathe Spirit-filled air together rather than alone. And as we walk in the Spirit's power side by side, we become more effective at representing Him in the world. That's because the Holy Spirit uses each one of us to build up the body of Christ through our individual gifts and abilities. That's the subject of our next chapter: How can we use our spiritual gifts to encourage and equip our fellow Christians?

REFLECTION QUESTIONS

1. Do you believe that the benefits of finding Christian community are worth the risk of hurt or rejection? Why or why not?
2. What is one step you can take to connect more closely with the body of Christ?

CHAPTER 9

The Gifts of the Spirit

*Each one should use whatever gift he
has received to serve others, faithfully
administering God's grace in its various forms.*

— 1 PETER 4:10

Every Christmas season, Shannon buys me a 1000-piece jig-saw puzzle with some seasonal image like a nativity scene, Santa Claus, or some beautiful winter landscape. The puzzle occupies my evenings for a couple of weeks. It's a stress reliev-er for me, something to take my mind off of the challenges of pastoral ministry.

Or at least it's a stress reliever most of the time. When a piece goes missing, my stress levels actually rise. It's horrible to put together 999 pieces, only to find out that you're missing one. I'm pretty good at regulating my emotions, but a misplaced puz-zle piece can bring me to tears.

If you're not a puzzle person, you might wonder why this is such a big deal. After all, 999 pieces are exactly where they belong. How important could one piece be when you have so many others? All I can say is that having a hole in your puzzle ruins the whole thing. There's no way to hide it, and there's no way to pretend it isn't there. Each piece is meant to fit in a particular place, and when one piece goes missing, the image is tarnished.

In some ways, the body of Christ is like a jigsaw puzzle. Every member has a role to play. The church is meant to be a living, breathing picture of Jesus Christ. When you first believed in Jesus, the Holy Spirit gave you gifts – abilities that God wants you to use to serve the church. Each one of our gifts is necessary for the church to reach its full potential. It's not that the church will fall apart or die if one person refuses to participate. After all, Jesus said that not even the gates of hell could overcome His church. But the absence of one person's gifts *can* keep the body of Christ from being as effective and spiritually mature as it's meant to be.

Not only will the church suffer, but our own spiritual lives will suffer. We're designed to be a part of Christ's mission in the world. We participate in that mission in part by using our spiritual gifts to serve the church. When we withhold our gifts from God's people, we're forfeiting the joy of making an impact on the lives of other Christians. Spirit-filled people will desire to use their spiritual gifts to serve the body of Christ.

"One person alone, no matter how gifted, cannot play
a Beethoven symphony, act a Shakespearian tragedy,
or compete against another team. The same is true
in the church. It can never be a solo performance."
—DAVID E. GARLAND[46]

Different Gifts, One Body

There are several New Testament passages that talk about spiritual gifts, but they all say basically the same thing: There is only one church, but many people with many different gifts. Every gift is necessary for the body of Christ to thrive. 1 Corinthians 12 is the most detailed passage in the New Testament on the subject of spiritual gifts. Notice how Paul describes the church as one body with many parts. Every part is different, but each one is equally important:

> *There are different kinds of gifts, but the same Spirit. There are different kinds of service, but the same Lord. There are different kinds of working, but the same God works all of them in all men. Now to each one the manifestation of the Spirit is given for the common good. To one there is given through the Spirit the message of wisdom, to another the message of knowledge by means of the same Spirit, to another faith by the same Spirit, to another gifts of healing by that one Spirit, to another miraculous powers, to another prophecy, to another distinguishing between spirits, to another speaking in different kinds of tongues, and to still another the interpretation of tongues. All these are the work of one and the same Spirit, and he gives them to each one, just as he determines. The body is a unit, though it is made up of many parts; and though all its parts are many, they form one body. So it is with Christ (1 Corinthians 12:4–12).*

Romans 12:4–8 is similar, but Paul uses a different list of spiritual gifts:

> *Just as each of us has one body with many members, and these members do not all have the same function, so in Christ we who are many form one body, and each member belongs to all the others. We have different gifts, according to the grace given us. If a man's gift is prophesying, let him use it in proportion to his faith. If it is serving, let him serve; if it is teaching, let him teach; if it is encouraging, let him encourage; if it is contributing to the needs of others, let him give generously; if it is leadership, let him govern diligently; if it is showing mercy, let him do it cheerfully.*

Ephesians 4:11–13 lists some positions of leadership that probably correspond with spiritual gifts. There is some overlap with the lists in 1 Corinthians 12 and Romans 12:

> *It was he who gave some to be apostles, some to be prophets, some to be evangelists, and some to be pastors and teachers, to prepare God's people for works of service, so that the body of Christ may be built up until we all reach unity in the faith and in the knowledge of the Son of God and become mature, attaining to the whole measure of the fullness of Christ.*

We learn a few important principles about spiritual gifts from these passages. First, every Christian has been given one or more spiritual gifts. Second, the Holy Spirit decides who gets which gifts. Third, not every Christian has the same gifts. Fourth, we're commanded to use our gifts to serve the church.

We need to answer an important question, though: What is a spiritual gift, anyway? And how does it differ from any other ability?

What is a Spiritual Gift?

Not long ago, my son's school invited some of its students to test for the "Gifted and Talented" program. When a school labels a child "gifted," what they normally mean is that he is unusually intelligent or creative. The word "gifted" in intriguing, though, because it implies that somebody (or Somebody?) gave you your abilities. If you're gifted, there must be a Giver. A particularly intelligent child, then, is academically gifted. An Olympic athlete might be considered athletically gifted. When rock guitarist Eddie Van Halen died, his friend Slash called him "a tremendously gifted musician."[47] Almost any extraordinary skill can be called a gift, and every good gift comes from God (James 1:17).

Spiritual gifts, though, are distinct from natural talents. For one thing, spiritual gifts are reserved for Christians, while natural abilities are given to everybody. For example, musical ability is a gift from God, but the Bible doesn't call it a spiritual gift. That's probably because anybody, whether they believe in Jesus or not, can be musically skilled. Spiritual gifts, on the other hand, are a type of ability that is only available to Christians. That's because only Christians are indwelt by the Holy Spirit.

Spiritual gifts are special manifestations of the Holy Spirit's life-giving breath. They are abilities that can only be explained by the Spirit's presence in our lives. You'll remember from chapter 3 that spiritual disciplines allow us to inhale the life-giving breath of God's Spirit. Spiritual gifts, though, allow us to *exhale* the Spirit's life-giving breath, for the benefit of the body of Christ.

The New Testament clearly describes spiritual gifts as supernatural abilities. While only some of them involve miraculous signs – gifts like healing and tongues – *all* of the spiritual gifts are supernatural. They only exist through the power of God's Spirit. A spiritual gift might overlap with a natural ability, of course; for example, the Spirit might use your natural intelligence to complement His gift of wisdom. But the two are still distinct. When we look at the lists of spiritual gifts in the New Testament, then, we need to avoid the mistake of calling some of them "supernatural" (e.g. healings and tongues) and some of them "natural" (wisdom, teaching, etc.).

That said, it's clear that some of the gifts involve miraculous signs, while others seem to be more common in the day-to-day ministry of the church. Take a look at the list below of all the spiritual gifts mentioned in the New Testament.

Wisdom	Prophecy	Service
Knowledge	Distinguishing of spirits	Encouragement
Faith	Tongues	Generosity
Healing	Interpretation of tongues	Leadership
Miracles	Teaching	Mercy
Administration	Helps	

That list is long, but it's probably not exhaustive. For example, it's likely that evangelism is a spiritual gift, since "evangelist" is listed as one of the positions of leadership in Ephesians 4:11. An evangelist is a person who is especially gifted for sharing the gospel with other people. You could say the same thing about pastoring (or shepherding) and apostleship. Those were offices in the early church that probably corresponded with spiritual gifts.

In addition, there are probably spiritual gifts that aren't listed anywhere in the New Testament. The writers of the Bible weren't trying to create a comprehensive list as a reference tool.

When they wrote about spiritual gifts, they were more concerned that Christians were using their gifts correctly, with the humility and faithfulness of Jesus.

"Some Christians struggle because they do not like the gifts, ministries, and or fruit that God has given them. They would prefer to have something else . . . I struggled with this issue, but eventually God gave me peace about my giftedness. I have learned that I can make the greatest contribution to the building of Christ's church by using what He has provided, not by insisting on serving Him as I prefer."

— THOMAS CONSTABLE[48]

Are the Sign Gifts Still Around?

One of the biggest debates among Christians is whether or not the sign gifts are still present in the church today. People also disagree about which gifts should be considered sign gifts, and which should not. However, it seems that the following spiritual gifts involve miraculous signs to one degree or another: healing, speaking in tongues, prophecy, and what Paul calls "miraculous powers" in 1 Corinthians 12.

Some Christians — often called cessationists — believe that these sign gifts were strictly reserved for the period of the early church when the gospel was still finding a foothold in the world. Cessationists believe that once the church was well-established, these sign gifts were no longer necessary. 1 Corinthians 13:8 is perhaps the most commonly-used passage to argue that those gifts no longer exist: *"Love never fails; but if there are gifts of prophecy, they will be done away; if there are tongues, they will cease; if there is knowledge, it will be done away."*

On the other end of the spectrum are Charismatic or Pentecostal Christians, who hold that the sign gifts still exist today, and that Christians should regularly practice them in the church. Some believe that *all* Christians should speak in tongues, and that speaking in tongues is the definitive sign that a person has been baptized by the Holy Spirit.

My own position falls in between. I don't believe that 1 Corinthians 13:8 teaches that sign gifts have been done away with today. Instead, I think that passage is describing Christ's future kingdom, when spiritual gifts will no longer be necessary at all. After all, we won't need miraculous signs to validate the gospel when Jesus is visibly ruling over the entire universe. However, I don't believe that miraculous signs are the ordinary way in which God works today. It seems clear from the Scripture that miracles and signs happened most frequently when God was doing something new in history – for example, when He was establishing the nation of Israel or validating the message of the gospel for the first time. I believe that sign gifts can still exist, but I think they are much more common in places where the gospel is relatively new – for example, in countries where missionaries are just beginning to share the gospel. Of course, the Holy Spirit can do whatever He wants, whether or not theologians agree with His methods.

Whatever your position on spiritual gifts, the important principle to remember is that they exist to build up the body of Christ and to glorify Jesus. That's really the main point of 1 Corinthians 13, the famous "love chapter." Paul says that miraculous gifts are of no value if they aren't practiced in love. If you can speak in tongues or perform miracles, but you're using those gifts to promote yourself rather than to build up the church, then your gifts won't have an eternal impact. Spiritual gifts exist to edify the body of Christ and to point people to Jesus. The gifts of the Spirit always ought to be guided by the fruit of the Spirit.

As we seek to discover our spiritual gifts, then, our primary goal ought to be to learn how we can encourage and build up the body of Christ. Rather than using our gifts to try to do something extraordinary or flashy, we'll use them to help others know Jesus better.

REFLECTION QUESTIONS

- Do you know your own spiritual gifts?
- Are you regularly using your spiritual gift(s) to serve the body of Christ? If not, why not?

How Can We Discover Our Gifts?

When I was in high school, every graduating senior had to take a vocational aptitude test. The goal of the test was to help us identify which career paths would fit our skills and interests. To be honest, I don't remember what the results of my test were. What I do remember is that a suspiciously high number of my classmates were told that they should become farmers. There's nothing wrong with farming, of course; it's a noble and necessary profession. But our high school was in suburban Dallas. Very few of us had any experience with farming. Most of us had never visited a farm, or even tried to grow tomatoes in the backyard. The idea that we were equipped to become farmers was laughable. We speculated that the test was secretly designed by the Department of Agriculture to remedy the nation's shortage of dedicated farmers.

That vocational aptitude test wasn't the best way to plot a career path. Similarly, I don't think that spiritual gifts tests are always the most effective way to discern how you should serve in the church. There are many such tests online, and they can be a helpful starting point for people (for example, churchgrowth.org has many such tests available for sale). They aren't bad tools for those who are unfamiliar with the concept of spiritual gifts, or who want a rough idea of the type of service opportunities they might be interested in pursuing.

Because spiritual gifts come from the Holy Spirit, though, I think the best way to discover our gifts is by means of the spiritual exercises we've talked about throughout this book. Read what the Bible says about spiritual gifts; pray that the Spirit will reveal your gifts to you; ask your Christian friends what they think your gifts are. Put yourself in a position to hear the Spirit's voice and He'll show you how you're gifted.

Once you've spent some time in prayer and listened to some wise counsel, I'd also encourage you to simply jump in and start serving your church. Ask your pastor or leadership team where people are needed; I'm sure they'll have some suggestions. Lead a Bible study to see if you're gifted to teach or join the parking team to find out if you have the gift of service. The great news is that you can't go wrong by serving God's people, even if you aren't particularly gifted in the area in which you serve. At worst, you'll learn something about yourself. Much more likely, you'll have a joyful experience, as you realize that you can contribute to the spiritual growth of the church, even in areas where you aren't particularly gifted. Over time, as you serve in a variety of ways, you'll come to better understand where you can contribute most effectively to the mission of the church.

"Many of us have never discovered or developed our spiritual gifts. There are spiritual resources within us which have never been tapped. They could transform your church and your life."
— WILLIAM MCRAE[49]

We Need You

One of the small tragedies in the way we approach church today is that people with more visible spiritual gifts, such as teaching or leadership, tend to receive more honor. But 1 Corinthians 12:22 tells us, *"the parts of the body that seem to be weaker are indispensable."* In other words, the church can't be healthy if the only people using their gifts are the people standing onstage. If you think your gifts aren't important simply because you serve behind the scenes, think again. The church needs you and your gifts. And you need to use your gifts; you'll become more like Jesus that way.

The church where I pastor met in a local elementary school for its first five years. During those years, I saw in unmistakable ways how the Holy Spirit uses every member of Christ's body to accomplish the church's mission. Every week we had to set up tons of equipment for our services: chairs, sound system, children's ministry rooms, welcome tables, and more. The job required dozens of volunteers and staff. While all of us contributed to the work, I could usually tell which people had the gift of service. Those men and women seemed to come alive at the thought of setting up chairs and tables so that we could worship

Jesus. I remember talking to one man who told me that serving on the setup team was the most meaningful spiritual experience he'd ever had. The Holy Spirit filled him with unbelievable joy as he used his spiritual gift of service.

Others with gifts of leadership and administration kept the whole operation running smoothly. They made sure that the teams showed up on time and knew exactly where to go and what to do. Those with the gift of encouragement walked through the halls while the work was going on, shouting, "Great work, everybody! Almost there! Think of all the people who will worship Jesus today because of what you're doing!" Those with the gift of generosity gave sacrificially so that we could purchase all that equipment in the first place, and many of those same men and women contributed when it was time to purchase the land for our permanent facility.

In a portable church setting, it was easy to see that all of our gifts were necessary for the church to fulfill its mission. Our goal was the same as that of any church: We wanted to help people find and follow Jesus. I have the gift of teaching, which is often more visible than other gifts, but there was no possible way I could've done everything by myself. My gifts might be more public than others, but they're no more important.

The beauty of the body of Christ is that as the Holy Spirit transforms us into Christ's image, He empowers us to serve the Lord together. While we can and should serve God individually, when we each use our gifts to build up the church, we paint a beautiful picture of the future kingdom of God.

As we connect with the church and use our gifts, we contribute to the mission of the church, as well. That's what we're going to discuss in the next chapter, as we approach the end of this book. As the Spirit of God transforms us, He sends us on a mission to invite more people to experience the meaning and joy that comes from knowing Jesus.

EXERCISE

- Ask a friend or spiritual mentor to tell you what they think your spiritual gift(s) are.
- If you aren't doing so already, find a place of service within your local church, where you can use your gifts to build up the body of Christ.

CHAPTER 10

The Spirit on Mission

"It is only the Spirit of God who enables one to carry on the redemptive mission of evangelism."

— ROBERT COLEMAN[50]

The 1990 film *Awakenings,* starring Robin Williams, tells the powerful story about a doctor who manages to "wake up" his catatonic patients, giving them a second chance at life. The movie is loosely based on the real-life story of Dr. Oliver Sacks. In the late 1960s, he discovered that the drug L-Dopa could successfully revive patients who had been rendered immobile by a form of encephalitis known as "sleeping sickness." People who couldn't communicate or even walk on their own were suddenly reanimated when they took L-Dopa. The transformation was sudden and dramatic. Unfortunately, it was also short-lived. Most patients who were treated with L-Dopa eventually returned to their catatonic state.

When I first saw the film, I found myself wondering what it would be like to suddenly awaken from the lethargy caused by catatonia. What would it be like to suddenly regain the ability to walk and talk, and to be able to communicate again with friends and loved ones? I can only imagine that it would feel like a resurrection of sorts, like you'd come back from the dead.

I find myself having the same reaction when I read the story of how the Holy Spirit first came to the earliest followers of Jesus. Acts 2 describes a powerful scene, in which the church suddenly came alive, full of new power and new abilities. They were able to communicate with God in a new way, and to fulfill His mission to an extent that was previously not possible for them. By now, you won't be surprised to read that when the Spirit showed up, He was accompanied by the sound of a "violent rushing wind." The Spirit's life-giving breath was so strong and powerful when He came upon the church that nothing was ever the same again. Read Acts 2:1–13 (NASB) and imagine what it must have been like to be present in that moment, when the Holy Spirit entered the church for the first time:

> *When the day of Pentecost came, they were all together in one place. Suddenly a sound like the blowing of a violent wind came from heaven and filled the whole house where they were sitting. They saw what seemed to be tongues of fire that separated and came to rest on each of them. All of them were filled with the Holy Spirit and began to speak in other tongues as the Spirit enabled them. Now there were staying in Jerusalem God-fearing Jews from every nation under heaven. When they heard this sound, a crowd came together in bewilderment, because each one heard them speaking in his own language. Utterly amazed, they asked: "Are not all these men who are speaking Galileans? Then how is it that each of us hears them in his own native language? Parthians, Medes and Elamites; residents of Mesopotamia, Judea and*

*Cappadocia, Pontus and Asia, Phrygia and Pamphylia,
Egypt and the parts of Libya near Cyrene; visitors from Rome
(both Jews and converts to Judaism); Cretans and Arabs—we
hear them declaring the wonders of God in our own tongues!"
Amazed and perplexed, they asked one another, "What does
this mean?" Some, however, made fun of them and said,
"They have had too much wine."*

The Holy Spirit's presence so dramatically changed these Christians that people mistook their transformation for drunkenness. We saw that same connection when we looked at Ephesians 5:18–19 earlier in this book, where Paul exhorted his readers not to be drunk with wine but instead to be filled with the Spirit.

Unlike alcohol, though, the Holy Spirit produces positive and permanent changes in our lives. The effects of alcohol eventually wear off, but the power of the Holy Spirit never does. For the early church, the Spirit's life-giving breath changed the way they approached their purpose in life, right from the moment He entered their midst. They realized that God was giving them a new and urgent mission, to make disciples of Jesus wherever they went.

---

*"What I enjoy so much about the ministry of multiplying
disciples is that it is scriptural and it works."*
— LEROY EIMS[51]

The Mission is Multiplication

If you have ever watched *Mission Impossible* – either the older television series or the newer movies – you know that the stories center on secret government spies who work for a fictional agency called the Impossible Mission Force, or IMF. At the beginning of every movie, the hero, Ethan Hunt, receives a recorded message describing his upcoming mission. The message always begins with the words, "Your mission, should you choose to accept it . . . " Presumably, Hunt has the option of refusing the mission, but I've never seen him do it. After all, if you decide to work for the Impossible Mission Force, you aren't very likely to refuse a dangerous (or even impossible) mission.

In the same way, Jesus didn't give His disciples an optional mission; He gave them a non-negotiable command. Matthew 28:18–20 records the final words Jesus spoke to His disciples before He ascended into heaven. This passage is commonly called The Great Commission. As many people have pointed out, it *isn't* called The Good Suggestion. Christ's mission is mandatory. Despite its importance, though, many Christians don't even know it exists. One recent survey found that 51% of American churchgoers are completely unfamiliar with the Great Commission![52] If you haven't heard of it, then, you're not alone. But it's important to understand what Jesus has asked His people to do, so let's take a look at Matthew 28:

> *Then Jesus came to them and said, "All authority in heaven and on earth has been given to me. Therefore go and make disciples of all nations, baptizing them in the name of the Father and of the Son and of the Holy Spirit, and teaching them to obey everything I have commanded you. And surely I am with you always, to the very end of the age."*

Jesus told His disciples that their mission in life was to make more disciples. They were supposed to multiply themselves, in other words. The word "disciple" in Greek refers to a student, or a learner. A disciple is somebody who learns from a particular teacher. But as you can see from Jesus' life, His disciples didn't simply sit in a classroom and listen to His teaching. They were also expected to follow Him around and do whatever He told them to do.

The final task that Jesus gave to His disciples was to go out into the world and teach *other* people how to follow Jesus. Christ's plan was that these new disciples would then make more disciples, who would then make even *more* disciples, and so on. Jesus intends for this task of spiritual multiplication to continue until He returns.

The New Testament makes it clear that the first disciples were completely focused on His mission. In the book of 2 Timothy, for example, the apostle Paul reiterated Jesus' commission to his young protégé Timothy:

> *The things which you have heard from me in the presence of many witnesses, entrust these to faithful men who will be able to teach others also* (2 Tim 2:2, NASB).

In this one verse, Paul mentions four generations of disciples: Paul himself, Timothy, the "faithful men" that Timothy was supposed to instruct, and the "others" that Timothy's disciples would then instruct. Paul was reminding Timothy that his job as a pastor was to actively participate in the Great Commission.

The Great Commission isn't only for pastors, though. *Every* Christian is commanded to tell people about Jesus (to evangelize) and to help them follow Jesus faithfully (to make disciples). When we do those things, the gospel will spread, the church will grow, and the nations will hear about Jesus. In fact, that's exactly what happened in the first century: The gospel spread rapidly, and within a few decades there were congregations of Jesus-followers all across the known world. In the book of Revelation, John wrote that heaven will one day be filled with men and women from *"every tribe, tongue, people, and nation"* (Revelation 5:9). The Great Commission is the means by which Jesus plans to bring people from every nation on earth into His eternal kingdom.

Of course, the success of the early church's mission was only made possible through the Holy Spirit's power. Jesus' disciples obeyed Him, but the Spirit was the one who changed people's hearts and drew them to Jesus. The Spirit did the real work of spiritual transformation. That's why the Holy Spirit is mentioned constantly in the book of Acts. In fact, no other book of the Bible mentions the Holy Spirit as often as the book of Acts; by my own count, Acts contains 56 references to the Holy Spirit. The crucial point here is that we will only be effective in fulfilling Jesus' mission when we're walking with the Spirit. Just as He breathes life into God's people, He breathes life into the church as a whole.

If we desire to see the world change, if we really hope to see men and women come to know Jesus from every nation on earth, then we must constantly pursue a life-giving relationship with the Holy Spirit. Only then will He fill us with His spiritual breath and provide us with the power we need to change the world.

We must be laser-focused on two goals: Knowing Jesus and making Him known to others. God will do extraordinary things through Spirit-filled people who wholeheartedly pursue the Great Commission. Of course, that's easier said than done.

There are a thousand ways to become distracted and to lose sight of our mission.

REFLECTION QUESTIONS

- When was the last time you shared the gospel with somebody who doesn't know Jesus?
- If somebody who knows you well were asked what they think is the mission of your life, what would they say? Would they say that knowing Jesus and helping others to know Him is the highest priority of your life? Why or why not?

Distractions Are Everywhere

One of my favorite stores is Lowe's, the enormous hardware and home improvement store. I go there often to buy tools and supplies for my household projects. Lowe's carries everything from light bulbs to jigsaws to major appliances. Of course, that's why I love it: They have a vast selection of cool home improvement products, and they rarely fail to stock whatever I need.

On the other hand, the store's greatest strength can also be my downfall. Quite often I go to Lowe's intending to get something as small as a Styrofoam faucet cover, but I come home with tools I didn't even know I "needed" before I walked in the door. There are so many delightful items to dazzle the eyes there, even though I don't need most of them, and I can't really afford them. If I'm not careful, I might forget why I came there in the first place. I could drive home with a brand-new hammer drill, but not with the faucet cover I really needed.

We face that same problem when it comes to the Great Commission. We know that our purpose in life is to make disciples, but there are so many other pursuits to distract us. The world is full of interesting opportunities and troubling concerns that have nothing to do with the mission of Jesus.

For example, many Christians get stressed about presidential elections, to the point of neglecting the Great Commission. Don't get me wrong, politics matters. Elections affect people's lives. But convincing our friends to vote for our candidate is *not* our life's mission. If we spend more time arguing about politics on social media than we do telling people about Jesus, that's proof positive that we're distracted from our primary mission.

Maybe politics aren't your downfall, but you are consumed with everyday concerns. Perhaps you're obsessed with having a perfect marriage or raising successful children. Marriage and children are good gifts from God, of course, but we need to ask ourselves *why* we care so much about our marriages and our families. In the final analysis, our families exist to bring glory to Jesus, so that people can know and understand who He is. Ephesians 5 tells us that our marriages exist to reflect the relationship between Christ and the church. That's the purpose of marriage. Similarly, the way we raise our children can be a picture of how God the Father relates to His children. In other words, we aren't meant to focus on our families to the exclusion of the Great Commission, but as a part of it.

That same principle also applies to building our careers. Our vocations exist to further God's purposes in the world, not our own. How can we use our jobs to bring glory to Jesus? How can our vocations help us as we seek to make disciples? When we pursue earthly goals for our own sake, they become distractions from the work that Jesus has called us to do. When we pursue those same goals for Jesus' sake, however, He will use us in amazing ways to fulfill His purposes in the world.

I believe that one of the reasons that Christians and churches are so divided today is because we're distracted from fulfilling the Great Commission. We argue over secondary issues because we aren't focused on what's most important. We argue over everything from politics to worship styles, and as a result, we lack the power and impact that Jesus wants us to have in the world.

This is not to suggest that we should ignore the problems of our society or turn a blind eye to matters of racial or economic injustice. Instead, we should engage in those discussions as a part of our mission, and not as an end in and of themselves. The coming kingdom of Jesus is a place where men and women from every tribe, tongue, people, and nation will worship Him side by side. Paul says in Galatians 3:28 that economic status, race, social class, and other earthly categories should not divide the body of Christ. For that reason, questions of race, economics, and justice matter immensely. We can't ignore them if we want to be faithful representatives of Christ's kingdom.

At the same time, we must remember that we are not here to build a particular earthly kingdom. We aren't here to shape our country or our world into what *we* think it ought to be. Instead, our mission in life – and in our churches – is to be ambassadors of Christ's perfect kingdom. As His representatives, we ought to constantly proclaim the good news that we worship a perfect and powerful King, and that He's coming back soon.

At the beginning of this book, I said that the church needs a new Reformation. At the heart of the Protestant Reformation was the conviction that the church had lost sight of the profound and life-transforming grace of God. The reality of the gospel needed to be recovered. It seems to me that the church is at a similar turning point today. We have lost sight of the centrality of the gospel and the importance of our mission. If we are going to have the power and impact that Jesus prayed the church would have, we must refocus our attention on the priorities of His kingdom. And we must constantly seek the Holy Spirit's power and wisdom to do God's will.

REFLECTION QUESTIONS

- What distractions are most likely to keep you personally from focusing on the Great Commission?
- What can you do to make sure that your life is centered on the mission of Jesus? Consider how the spiritual breathing exercises we have studied in this book might help.

The Spirit Paves the Way

Perhaps the most encouraging part of the Great Commission is at the end, when Jesus says, *"I am with you always, even to the end of the age."* Of course, immediately after saying that, Jesus ascended into heaven. I used to wonder why Jesus left the planet immediately after promising that He'd always be with us. But I know now, of course, that Jesus didn't actually leave us. He is still with us, through the presence of the Holy Spirit.

Jesus wanted His disciples to know that the Holy Spirit would always pave the way for them. Their mission would not be an easy one, but they would not be alone in it. The life-giving breath of the Spirit would fill their hearts and give them the strength they needed for the task ahead. They wouldn't have to be afraid of anything because God would always be with them.

When I was a child, one of my daily chores was to empty the skimmer baskets next to our family's swimming pool. If you don't know what skimmers are, they're just baskets along the side of the pool where leaves and debris are collected. The baskets need to be emptied regularly in order to keep the pool clean. But one of our skimmers was behind a very large evergreen tree in the backyard, and I was terrified to walk behind that tree in the dark. I was afraid that there were villains and monsters hiding back there. I had nightmares about it, in fact. So I asked my dad to come outside and watch me while I emptied the skimmers. Knowing that he was out there with me gave me the courage to finish the chore. After all, if my dad was right there, I knew the monsters wouldn't attack me.

In the same way, the Holy Spirit's presence gave Jesus' disciples the courage that they didn't have before He came. During Christ's life, Peter was a fearful man who was often afraid to stand up for what was right. But after Christ's resurrection, on the Day of Pentecost, he was like a completely different person (Acts 2). He stood in front of thousands of people and boldly proclaimed the gospel. He willingly endured imprisonment and persecution for the name of Christ. Nothing distracted him from the mission of Jesus, and nothing seemed to scare him. What made such a dramatic difference? What gave Peter and his fellow disciples such courage and perseverance? The Holy Spirit. He changed everything. And if the Spirit gave that power to the first disciples, He can give it to us as well.

Make no mistake, the Great Commission is a scary mission. We might be rejected or persecuted for preaching the gospel. But Jesus promised to be with us. He promised that the Spirit would never leave us (Romans 8:10–11). The Spirit will go ahead of us, convicting men and women of their sin and their need for a Savior (John 16:8). He provides us with the power and wisdom that we need to share the gospel clearly and confidently. We're never alone as we fulfill Christ's mission.

I'll say this once more: The Holy Spirit wants to give us lives of joy and purpose beyond anything we can imagine. He wants to transform our hearts and use us to transform the world itself. So, are you ready to participate in the greatest mission in all of human history? Are you ready to make an impact for Christ's kingdom through the transforming power of the Holy Spirit? If you are, let me offer some practical ways to get started.

Where Do We Begin?

Hopefully, you're convinced by now that the Great Commission is worth your time, energy, and money. You believe that when you cultivate a life-transforming relationship with the Spirit, He will empower you to make disciples. You really can impact the world for Christ! If you're ready to get started, let me offer six practical suggestions:

- *Learn.* If you were unfamiliar with the Great Commission before reading this chapter, you know what it is now. But there's still much more to learn. The Great Commission is a worldwide task. There are places around the world where churches are so rare that the average person will never even see one. In some countries, there are so few Christians that most people will never meet one. And of course, there are countless people living in our own neighborhoods who lack the hope that only Jesus can provide. The more we learn about the state of the world, the more the Spirit will convict us to pray and to participate in the Great Commission. If you're interested in learning more about the state of the Great Commission around the world, one great resource is the Joshua Project (www.joshuaproject. net). They provide statistics and information about the spiritual state of every nation in the world. If you'd like some help making disciples closer to home, I highly recommend the classic book *The Master Plan of Evangelism* by Robert Coleman. His book explains how Jesus made disciples, and it provides excellent suggestions for how to do so yourself.

- *Pray.* As you deepen your prayer life, you'll want to pray regularly for those who don't know Jesus. Pray for your friends and family members, of course, but also pray for the world. Use your prayer chart to help you pray for different people and nations each day. When you go to work, or interact with your neighbors, or visit your favorite coffee shop, pray for an opportunity to share the good news of Jesus. Think about specific people you know who need to know Jesus and pray that they will have receptive hearts and minds. Ask the Holy Spirit to give you wisdom and boldness to tell them about Christ.

- *Speak.* Not long ago, I asked my friends on Facebook to share with me some subject that they could talk about for hours, even if their friends grew bored with it. I was amazed to hear the many interests my friends had: pop music, movies, computers, the British Monarchy, Civil War history, and so many other subjects. You name it and it's somebody's pet subject. When we're truly excited about something, we can't seem to stop talking about it. It's interesting, though, that when it comes to the gospel, we're often afraid to speak. We're willing to risk sounding strange when we talk about our earthly interests, but when it comes to sharing the greatest news in the universe, we suddenly clam up.

Despite my fears, I've found that most people aren't offended by spiritual questions. If the subject of Jesus is approached with kindness and respect, most people are willing to talk about Him. If we are walking with the Spirit on a daily basis, He will give us the wisdom and gentleness that we need to start these conversations. We don't have to be afraid; after all, the Spirit that raised Jesus from the dead lives inside of us (Romans 8:11)! As you pray for your friends and family members who need to know Jesus, pray that you will have the courage to *"make a defense to everyone who asks you to give an account for the hope that is in you, yet with gentleness and reverence"* (1 Peter 3:15).

If you don't feel qualified to share the gospel, check out the book *The 7 Principles of an Evangelistic Life* by Douglas Cecil. Dr. Cecil gives some great tips for how to strike up spiritual conversations, and how to present the gospel clearly. He explains that any good gospel presentation includes three essential truths: (1) Everybody is a sinner, and sin keeps all of us from having a relationship with God; (2) Jesus died to pay the penalty for our sins, and then He rose from the dead; and (3) Everybody who believes in Jesus is forgiven of their sins and receives eternal life. It's simple, easy to understand, and anybody can learn to share it.[53]

- *Train.* Once a person has trusted in Jesus, of course, their walk with Him has only just begun. Every Christian needs to learn how to follow Him on a daily basis. They need to know how to live a Spirit-filled life, and how to make disciples themselves. No matter where you are in your own spiritual journey, you can invest in the lives of other Christians. Perhaps this book could get them started. Every Christian ought to be actively training at least one or two other Christians to know Jesus deeper and to share Him with others. We are all commanded to participate in the process of spiritual multiplication.

  Think about your relationships and identify two or three people that you can train to know Jesus in a deeper way. Maybe your church has high-school or college students who want to know Jesus better. Or maybe you have a friend who recently trusted Jesus and wants to understand more about God and His Word. Everyone has different needs, so you will need to pray and find the appropriate resources. If you're looking for some help to get started, check out www.grace-bible.org/disciplemaker. My church has a number of free resources at that link that will help you become a more effective disciple-maker.

- *Give.* The early Christians were incredibly generous. They gave of their money and resources to support one another (Acts 2:44–45), but they also gave money toward the spread of the gospel. The entire book of Philippians is essentially a thank-you note from the apostle Paul, because the church in Philippi gave money to support his missionary work (see Philippians 4:10–19). The Scripture repeatedly affirms that the Great Commission is worth not only our time and energy, but also our money. Every

Christian is called to make disciples, but we are also called to contribute to the needs of those who are making disciples all around the world.

You can begin by giving money to your local church. Hopefully, your church uses its resources to further the Great Commission. Many churches have local outreach ministries, designed to share the gospel and help people in need. Many churches also have a missions budget for supporting overseas missionaries. By giving to your church, you can help fulfill the Great Commission.

You can also give directly toward international missionaries and local outreach organizations. My own family has had the opportunity to support a number of people who live and work overseas, sharing the gospel in places where churches are scarce. We've also had the chance to support local outreach ministries right here in our own community. While I hope that our financial gifts are helpful to them, our family also benefit as we pray for what God is doing all around the world. In that way, the Spirit changes our hearts when we decide to use our financial resources to further the gospel.

- *Go.* Finally, consider whether the Spirit is calling *you* to leave your comfort zone and go to another country or another culture to share the gospel. For some people, that will involve going on a short-term mission trip to assist the work of long-term missionaries. For others, that could mean moving overseas for a season – or even permanently – to become a full-time missionary. Every time I go on a mission trip, the Holy Spirit works at least as profoundly in my own heart as He does in the lives of those I minister to. When we engage with another culture for the sake of the Great Commission, the Holy Spirit broadens our perspective and we begin to understand that we're just one small part of the work that God is doing in the world.

The Great Adventure

For those first disciples of Jesus, there was never any question that they would actively participate in the Great Commission. When the Holy Spirit entered their hearts, they became captivated by Christ's mission. After all, Jesus was alive and He'd given their lives hope and new meaning. How could they possibly use their lives for some lesser purpose?

When they were afraid and discouraged, and when they faced persecution and even death, they remembered Jesus' promise to always be with them. That same promise still holds true. Jesus will be with us, *"even to the end of the age."* The Spirit of God, God's life-giving breath, empowers us for this mission. Now that we know Him, we can follow Him boldly on this great adventure of making disciples. We can set aside every distraction and hindrance and run our race with endurance and hope (Hebrews 12:1–2). Until Jesus returns, His Spirit will continue to transform our hearts and to empower us to do God's will. And as we listen closely to His voice, our lives will have more joy and purpose than we can possibly imagine.

EXERCISE

Take a few minutes right now and ask the Spirit to show you one concrete way to participate in the Great Commission. Use the suggestions above as a starting point. Then tell Him you will follow wherever He leads you, trusting Him for courage and wisdom.

Do You Believe Change is Possible?

One January several years ago, I joined a gym as part of a New Year's Resolution to get healthier. I attended a "boot camp" class the first week that nearly made me give up on my resolution. At the time I was forty years old and I hadn't exercised consistently for several years. During that first class the instructor had us do something like 120 push-ups, 50 squats, 50 sit-ups, and 100 ball slams, along with riding on a terrible stationary bike, aptly named "the assault bike." Don't feel bad if some of those exercises are unfamiliar to you because they were to me also. The point is that I was woefully out of shape. I failed to complete all of the exercises, mostly because I kept running out of breath. I lacked the lung capacity I needed for such strenuous exercise.

It was only the encouragement of the instructor that kept me going. I don't remember her exact words, but she said something like, "You did alright for your first class. But if you come back regularly, you'll get stronger. And as you get stronger, these exercises won't be as foreign or as difficult." Although I suspected she was mostly being nice – and maybe trying not to lose a client – I decided to take her at her word. I set a goal to show up at least three times a week for the next several months. It turned out that the instructor was right. The first few weeks were still quite difficult, but I felt my muscles slowly growing stronger. I ran slightly faster, and I didn't run out of air quite as quickly. Don't get me wrong: I was far from the strongest or fastest person at the gym but showing up day in and day out actually began to change my body. I became better able to take in the air that I needed to finish all of the exercises. Consistency produced transformation.

The same principle applies when it comes to walking with the Spirit. If we want to learn how to breathe spiritually, we must practice, day in and day out, year after year. At first, we will struggle to hear His voice. We will wonder if anything is really happening when we pray, or if our hearts are truly being transformed by God's Word. We might question whether spiritual change is actually possible, or whether we can actually have an impact for Christ's kingdom. We won't yet have the spiritual lung capacity that we need to do all that God is calling us to do.

Over time, though, we will learn how to fill our lungs with the breath of God's Spirit. When we are stressed, or tempted, or tired, our lives will start to yield the fruit of the Spirit instead of the deeds of the flesh. When the voices of the world threaten to drown out the voice of Jesus, we will learn how to sing praises in the face of despair. When we are distracted by the pleasures or the struggles of this world, we will learn how to remain focused on the Great Commission. We will realize that the Spirit who raised Jesus from the dead is with us every moment, living inside of us and transforming us into Christ's image. And

He will give us the strength and endurance to help others, as well. Our lives will make an impact as we encourage others to breath the life-giving air of His Spirit.

You and I might not ever be famous like Corrie ten Boom or George Mueller, but that's alright. Remember, the life-giving breath of the Spirit isn't only for extraordinary Christians, but also for ordinary Christians like you and me. We will never know on this side of heaven what the impact of our lives will be when we listen to the Spirit's voice and obey Him on a daily basis. What we know is that God wants to use our lives in ways that we cannot even imagine.

My prayer is that you and I will truly believe that the Holy Spirit wants to lead you to a life of purpose and joy beyond your wildest dreams. I pray that we will believe that He truly wants to change everything for us, and that only He has the power to do so. The question is whether you and I will consistently put ourselves in a position where we can hear and respond to His voice. Will we fill our lungs with His breath and trust the Lord to do great work, both in us and through us? May God give you His Spirit's power and grace as you learn to follow in the footsteps of His Son Jesus.

A Note from the Author

Thank you for reading this book! If you enjoyed it, would you take a moment to leave a review on Amazon? Your review will help other people find this resource and benefit from it.

If you'd like to contact me, you can reach out in any of the following ways:

Website: www.mattmorton.net (subscribe for email updates and helpful resources designed to help you walk by the Spirit)

Instagram: @pastormattmorton
Twitter: @MatthewRMorton

You can also find more information and resources from Grace Bible Church in College Station, Texas at www.grace-bible.org.

Acknowledgements

Thank you to the following people, without whom this book would not be possible.

To my wife Shannon, who believed in this project from the beginning, and has always encouraged me to continue writing, even when the work is hard and the rewards are few. I love you.

Elizabeth, Abby, and Sam, who have taught me a great deal about how to know Jesus and to walk with the Holy Spirit.

My mom, Debi Morton, who has taught me so much about prayer and about the Spirit-filled life.

Brian Fisher, who has shaped my theology and understanding of the Christian faith more than nearly anyone else I know.

Bruce Barbour, who encouraged this project and helped shepherd it to completion.

Dusty Davis, Chris Thompson, Gavin Sledge, Ben Clausen, Katie Coyle, Whitney Kriel, Jenn Chalmers, Grace Bumguardner, Karyleigh Olson, Elliot Matson, Julie Beth Craig, and all the staff of Grace Creekside, for serving Jesus faithfully with me.

Amber Roberts and David Morton, who read an early version of this manuscript and provided helpful feedback.

Ben Stuart and Blake Jennings, for being the sort of friends who help me walk with the Spirit.

The elders, leaders, and all of the men and women of Grace Bible Church. My thoughts about the Holy Spirit have been shaped and refined by your influence and encouragement.

Studying the Bible

The method of Bible study that I've found most effective in my own life is called inductive Bible study. Instead of approaching the Bible with a preconceived notion of what it means and how to apply it to our lives, we begin by letting the Scripture speak first. We read each passage in its context to determine what it actually says. We ask the question, "What do I see?" (Observation). Then we ask, "What does this mean?" (Interpretation). Finally, we ask, "How should I apply this to my life?" (Application). As I mentioned in Chapter 4, if you're looking for a more thorough discussion of this method, you'll want to get a copy of *Living by the Book* by Howard and William Hendricks. It's an excellent resource. In addition, you can go to www.grace-bible.org for some studies on specific books of the Bible that follow this method. Below is a summary of the inductive Bible study method to get you started.

Step 1: Observation

Before we can determine what a passage means, we must first figure out what it actually says. We want to ask the question,

"What do I see?" Here are some questions to ask about every passage when you're making observations:

1. Who is the speaker? Who is the audience? Who is the writer?
2. When did the events take place, or when was this written? (Note: You might need to pick up a Bible dictionary or commentary to answer this).
3. Where did this take place, or where was it written? Where are the characters coming from or going?
4. What is occurring in this passage?
5. How is the action being accomplished? What is the order of events (especially if it's a narrative passage)?
6. Why is this action happening, or why did the author write these words?
7. Are there comparison words ("like" or "as")? What is being compared?
8. Are there contrast words ("but")?
9. What words or thoughts are repeated more than once?
10. Does this material reach a climax (especially in a narrative)?
11. Are there causation words ("therefore," "because") or substantiation words ("so that")?
12. Are there other explanatory words ("for," "as a result")?
13. Are there conditional words and phrases ("if")?

Everything is fair game when you're making observations. No observation is too small or too obvious. Some people find it's helpful to circle verbs, or put a box around nouns, or to underline adjectives and adverbs, and so on. That way you can get a sense of the structure of each sentence or phrase as you observe the details of the passage.

Step 2: Interpretation

In this stage of the process, you're asking the question, "What does this mean?" There are a number of skills you can use to accomplish this. There are also some great online tools, such as www.biblestudytools.com.

- Study individual words and what they mean. See where else a particular word is used in the Bible. For example, if you see the word "salvation" in your passage, get a concordance and look at every time that word is used in the New Testament. How is this word used? What do you think it means in your particular context?
- Look at the context carefully. Is there anything in the verses that precede or follow your passage that helps you understand it better?
- Look at cross-references. Are there other passages that are similar to the one you're reading? That might shed light on the meaning of your passage (for example, Ephesians 5:15–21 is quite similar to Colossians 3:12–17). Many English Bibles include cross-references in the margins.
- Compare multiple translations. Sometimes you might notice slight differences between the translations that help you understand the meaning of a passage better.
- Read and study background information. Knowing more about the audience, the author, the time period, the location, the situation, and so on can provide insight into a passage. Use a good Bible dictionary or background

commentary. Software programs such as Logos also contain excellent resources for background information.

- <u>Ask and answer important interpretive questions</u>. For example, you might wonder about the meaning of the word "save" in a tough passage like James 2:14. After studying other places where the word is used, list the possibilities. Then choose the most likely option, based on your study and the context. You might not have complete certainty but doing the work of study can help you get closer.

Your primary goal in this step is to determine what the original author meant, as closely as possible. Once you know what the passage actually means, then you can ask the final question as you move toward application.

Step 3: Application

This is the step where we ask, "How does this apply to me?" Based on the passage's meaning, do the following:

- <u>List important principles</u>. Is there a command in this passage for me to obey? Is there something about God's character that leads me to worship Him? Is there something about my relationships with other people that requires me to change some things? Are there promises that God wants me to trust?
- <u>Choose one or two principles to focus on</u>. You can't change everything all at once. Select one or two principles to really focus on as you seek to follow Jesus more closely. Pray that the Spirit will transform your heart and your actions as you listen closely to God's Word.

52 Key Memory Verses by Topic

(Bible Quotes from NASB)

The Gospel

For God so loved the world that he gave his one and only Son, that whoever believes in him shall not perish but have eternal life. (John 3:16)

He himself bore our sins in his body on the tree, so that we might die to sins and live for righteousness; by his wounds you have been healed. (1 Peter 2:24)

For what I received I passed on to you as of first importance, that Christ died for our sins according to the Scriptures, that he was buried, that he was raised on the third day according to the Scriptures. (1 Corinthians 15:3–4)

And this is the testimony, God has given us eternal life, and this life is in his Son. He who has the Son has life; he who does not have the Son of God does not have life. (1 John 5:11–12)

But God demonstrates his own love for us in this, While we were still sinners, Christ died for us. (Romans 5:8)

Faith

However, to the man who does not work but trusts God who justifies the wicked, his faith is credited as righteousness. (Romans 4:5)

I am not ashamed of the gospel, because it is the power of God for the salvation of everyone who believes, first for the Jew, then for the Gentile. (Romans 1:16)

Whoever believes in the Son has eternal life, but whoever rejects the Son will not see life, for God's wrath remains on him. (John 3:36)

Grace

For it is by grace you have been saved, through faith—and this not from yourselves, it is the gift of God— not by works, so that no one can boast. (Ephesians 2:8–9)

For the grace of God that brings salvation has appeared to all men. (Titus 2:11)

The law was added so that the trespass might increase. But where sin increased, grace increased all the more, so that, just as sin reigned in death, so also grace might reign through righteousness to bring eternal life through Jesus Christ our Lord. (Romans 5:20–21)

For all have sinned and fall short of the glory of God and are justified freely by his grace through the redemption that came by Christ Jesus. (Romans 3:23–24)

Jesus is God

In the beginning was the Word, and the Word was with God, and the Word was God. (John 1:1)

The Son is the radiance of God's glory and the exact representation of his being, sustaining all things by his powerful word. After he had provided purification for sins, he sat down at the right hand of the Majesty in heaven. (Hebrews 1:3)

For in Christ all the fullness of the Deity lives in bodily form. (Colossians 2:9)

God's Word

All Scripture is God-breathed and is useful for teaching, rebuking, correcting and training in righteousness, so that the man of God may be thoroughly equipped for every good work. (2 Timothy 3:16–17)

Above all, you must understand that no prophecy of Scripture came about by the prophet's own interpretation. For prophecy never had its origin in the will of man, but men spoke from God as they were carried along by the Holy Spirit. (2 Peter 1:20–21)

I tell you the truth, until heaven and earth disappear, not the smallest letter, not the least stroke of a pen, will by any means disappear from the Law until everything is accomplished. (Matthew 5:18)

Heaven and earth will pass away, but my words will never pass away. (Matthew 24:35)

God's Love

Greater love has no one than this, that he lay down his life for his friends. (John 15:13)

For I am convinced that neither death nor life, neither angels nor demons, neither the present nor the future, nor any powers, neither height nor depth, nor anything else in all creation, will be able to separate us from the love of God that is in Christ Jesus our Lord. (Romans 8:38–39)

Dear friends, let us love one another, for love comes from God. Everyone who loves has been born of God and knows God. Whoever does not love does not know God, because God is love. (1 John 4:7–8)

Holy Spirit

But the fruit of the Spirit is love, joy, peace, patience, kindness, goodness, faithfulness, gentleness and self-control. Against such things there is no law. (Galatians 5:22–23)

But the Counselor, the Holy Spirit, whom the Father will send in my name, will teach you all things and will remind you of everything I have said to you. (John 14:26)

The Spirit gives life; the flesh counts for nothing. The words I have spoken to you are spirit and they are life. (John 6:63)

And if the Spirit of him who raised Jesus from the dead is living in you, he who raised Christ from the dead will also give life to your mortal bodies through his Spirit, who lives in you. (Romans 8:11)

The Spirit himself testifies with our spirit that we are God's children. (Romans 8:16)

For we were all baptized by one Spirit into one body—whether Jews or Greeks, slave or free—and we were all given the one Spirit to drink. (1 Corinthians 12:13)

Prayer

Pray without ceasing. (1 Thessalonians 5:17)

Be joyful in hope, patient in affliction, faithful in prayer. (Romans 12:12)

Do not be anxious about anything, but in everything, by prayer and petition, with thanksgiving, present your requests to God. And the peace of God, which transcends all understanding, will guard your hearts and your minds in Christ Jesus. (Philippians 4:6–7)

Therefore confess your sins to each other and pray for each other so that you may be healed. The prayer of a righteous man is powerful and effective. (James 5:16)

If any of you lacks wisdom, he should ask God, who gives generously to all without finding fault, and it will be given to him. (James 1:5)

The Great Commission/Discipleship

Then Jesus came to them and said, "All authority in heaven and on earth has been given to me. Therefore go and make disciples of all nations, baptizing them in the name of the Father and of the Son and of the Holy Spirit, and teaching them to obey everything I have commanded you. And surely I am with you always, to the very end of the age." (Matthew 28:18–20)

And the things you have heard me say in the presence of many witnesses entrust to reliable men who will also be qualified to teach others. (2 Timothy 2:2)

The Greatest Commandment

Jesus replied, "'Love the Lord your God with all your heart and with all your soul and with all your mind.' This is the first and greatest commandment. And the second is like it, 'Love your neighbor as yourself.' All the Law and the Prophets hang on these two commandments." (Matthew 22:37–40)

Holiness

But just as he who called you is holy, so be holy in all you do; for it is written, "Be holy, because I am holy." (1 Peter 1:15–16)

Make every effort to live in peace with all men and to be holy; without holiness no one will see the Lord. (Hebrews 12:14)

Your Thought Life

Finally, brothers, whatever is true, whatever is noble, whatever is right, whatever is pure, whatever is lovely, whatever is admirable—if anything is excellent or praiseworthy—think about such things. (Philippians 4:8)

Your Words

Do everything without complaining or arguing, so that you may become blameless and pure, children of God without fault in a crooked and depraved generation, in which you shine like stars in the universe. (Philippians 2:14–15)

Let your conversation be always full of grace, seasoned with salt, so that you may know how to answer everyone. (Colossians 4:6)

Loving Others

This is the message you heard from the beginning; We should love one another. (1 John 3:11)

A new command I give you, Love one another. As I have loved you, so you must love one another. By this all men will know that you are my disciples if you love one another. (John 13:34–35)

Forgiving Others

Be kind and compassionate to one another, forgiving each other, just as in Christ God forgave you. (Ephesians 4:32)

Endurance

Let us not become weary in doing good, for at the proper time we will reap a harvest if we do not give up. (Galatians 6:9)

Therefore, since we are surrounded by such a great cloud of witnesses, let us throw off everything that hinders and the sin that so easily entangles, and let us run with perseverance the race marked out for us. Let us fix our eyes on Jesus, the author and perfecter of our faith, who for the joy set before him endured the cross, scorning its shame, and sat down at the right hand of the throne of God. (Hebrews 12:1–2)

Consider it pure joy, my brothers, whenever you face trials of many kinds, because you know that the testing of your faith develops perseverance. Perseverance must finish its work so that you may be mature and complete, not lacking anything. (James 1:2–4)

Joy

Rejoice in the Lord always. I will say it again, Rejoice! (Philippians 4:4)

Rejoice always! (1 Thessalonians 5:16)

Confession of Sin

If we confess our sins, He is faithful and righteous to forgive us our sins and to cleanse us from all unrighteousness. (1 John 1:9)

Christ's Return

For our citizenship is in heaven, from which also we eagerly wait for a Savior, the Lord Jesus Christ. (Philippians 3:20)

He who testifies to these things says, "Yes, I am coming quickly." Amen. Come, Lord Jesus. (Revelation 22:20)

Prayer Chart

Note that this is just a suggested template. The categories and specifics will change according to your own prayer needs and requests. In addition, you will need to periodically update the chart, since needs and requests will change. On the following page, there is a blank chart for you to fill in on your own.

	Monday	Tuesday	Wednesday	Thursday	Friday	Saturday	Sunday
Me	Wisdom	Patience					
Spouse							
Children	Sarah, health	Will, obedience					
Christian friends							
Non-Christian friends	Erin, to know Jesus						
Church							
Community							
World							

	Monday	Tuesday	Wednesday	Thursday	Friday	Saturday	Sunday
Me							
Spouse							
Children							
Christian friends							
Non-Christian friends							
Church							
Community							
World							

Notes

1. Sider, Ronald J. *The Scandal of the Evangelical Conscience: Why Are Christians Living Just like the Rest of the World?* Baker Books, 2005.

2. Barna Group. *Gen Z, Vol. 2.* Barna Group, 2021, pp. 61-65.

3. Chan, Francis, and Danae Yankoski. *Forgotten God: Reversing Our Tragic Neglect of the Holy Spirit.* David C. Cook, 2015.

4. Brooks, S. (2020, February 06). 107-Year-Old Sarasota man still living life to the fullest with fiancée and driver's license. Retrieved February 19, 2021, from https://www.wfla.com/news/wfla-plus/107-year-old-sarasota-man-still-living-life-to-the-fullest-with-fiance-and-drivers-license/

5. Ryrie, Charles Caldwell. *A Survey of Bible Doctrine.* Moody Pr., 1973, p. 67.

6 Erickson, Millard J. *Christian Theology.* Baker Book House, 1985, p. 862.

7. Weber, J. (2018, October 16). Christian, what do you believe? Survey says probably a heresy about Jesus. Retrieved February 19, 2021, from https://www.christianitytoday.com/news/2018/october/what-do-christians-believe-ligonier-state-theology-heresy.html

8. Henry, M. (1994). *Matthew Henry's commentary on the whole Bible: complete and unabridged in one volume* (p. 4). Peabody: Hendrickson.

9. For a wonderful discussion of the Trinity, see Michael Reeves' excellent book, *Delighting in the Trinity* (IVP, 2012).

10. Hodge, C. (1997). Systematic theology (Vol. 1, p. 529). Oak Harbor, WA: Logos Research Systems, Inc.

11. Luther, M. (1998). *Commentary on the Epistle to the Galatians.* Project Gutenberg.

12. Galatians. (n.d.). Retrieved February 18, 2021, from https://www.planobiblechapel.org/tcon/notes/html/nt/galatians/galatians.htm

13. Wiersbe, W. W. (1996). *The Bible exposition commentary* (Vol. 1, p. 355). Wheaton, IL: Victor Books.

14. Luther, M. (1998). *Commentary on the Epistle to the Galatians.* Project Gutenberg.

15. "I will always love you." (2021, February 16). Retrieved February 19, 2021, from https://en.wikipedia.org/wiki/I_Will_Always_Love_You

16. Stanford marshmallow experiment. (2021, February 12). Retrieved February 19, 2021, from https://en.wikipedia.org/wiki/Stanford_marshmallow_experiment#cite_note-Shoda1990-5

17. Spurgeon, Charles Haddon. "The Sword of the Spirit." *The Spurgeon Center,* 19 Apr. 1891, www.spurgeon.org/resource-library/sermons/the-sword-of-the-spirit/#flipbook/.

18. "The Bible in America: 6-Year Trends." Barna Group, www.barna.com/research/the-bible-in-america-6-year-trends/.

19. "Americans Are Fond of the Bible, Don't Actually Read It." *Lifeway Research,* 11 Feb 2021, lifewayresearch.com/2017/04/25/lifeway-research-americans-are-fond-of-the-bible-don't-actually-read-it/.

20. My friend John Dyer has created a great online tool for generating a Bible-reading plan, https://j.hn/bible-reading-plan-generator/

21. Hendricks, Howard G. *Living by the Book: with Workbook.* Moody Press, 2014, page 22.

22. In Appendix 2, I've included a list of 52 memory verses arranged by topic. One good goal is to memorize one each week throughout the year.

23. Wallace, Daniel B. *Greek Grammar beyond the Basics: an Exegetical Syntax of the New Testament.* Zondervan, 2008, p. 639. Wallace states that either option is possible, but he ultimately decides in favor of singing being a result of being filled with the Spirit. I'm arguing here that singing is a result of being filled with the Spirit, but also a way we become filled with Him. Part of my reasoning is based on Colossians 3:16, a parallel passage in which being full of the "word" of Christ is accomplished by teaching one another and singing to one another.

24. Crowder, David. *Praise Habit: Finding God in Sunsets and Sushi.* NavPress, 2004.

25. Merker, Matt, and J. Ligon Duncan. *Corporate Worship: How the Church Gathers as God's People.* Crossway, 2021, p. 136.

26 One such artist is Sandra McCracken, whose "Psalms" album can be found on any streaming platform.

27. Benge, J., & Benge, G. (2014). *George Muller: The guardian of Bristol's orphans.* Seattle, WA: YWAM Pub, pp. 165-168.

28. Willard, Dallas. *The Spirit of the Disciplines: Understanding How God Changes Lives.* Family Christian Press, 2001, p. 186.

29. Foster, Richard J. *Celebration of Discipline: the Path to Spiritual Growth.* HarperOne, 2018, p. 33.

30. Yancey, Philip. *PRAYER: Does It Make Any Difference?* Zondervan, 2016, page 15.

31. Green-McAfee, J. (2018, June 05). The praying example of Susanna Wesley. Retrieved March 02, 2021, from https://www.faithgateway.com/praying-example-susanna-wesley/#.YD22g5NKiHE

32. Chan, Francis, and Danae Yankoski. *Forgotten God: Reversing Our Tragic Neglect of the Holy Spirit.* David C Cook, 2015, page 109.

33. *44 Smartphone Addiction Statistics for 2021.* (2021, January 4). SlickText. https://www.slicktext.com/blog/2019/10/smartphone-addiction-statistics/

34. McHugh, Adam S. *The Listening Life: Embracing Attentiveness in a World of Distraction.* IVP Books, 2015, p. 81.

35 Yancey, 170-171.

36. Constable, Thomas. *Romans*, www.planobiblechapel.org/tcon/notes/html/nt/romans/romans.htm.

37 The line, "For thine is the kingdom and the power and the glory forever. Amen," is not found in the oldest and most reliable Greek manuscripts of the New Testament, and therefore was probably not a part of the original prayer that Jesus prayed. While the line is consistent with the spirit of Christ's prayer, it was likely added later.

38. Ross, Alexander. *The Epistles of James and John.* W.B. Eerdmans, 1974, p. 146.

39. Foster, Richard J. *Celebration of Discipline: the Path to Spiritual Growth.* HarperOne, 2018, p. 153.

40. Ortlund, Dane C. *Gentle and Lowly: The Heart of Christ for Sinners and Sufferers.* Crossway Books, 2021, p. 194.

41. Satan's name actually comes from the Hebrew word for "accuser," and accusing God's people is one of the main things that he does. For example, read Job 1 and Zechariah 3:1.

42. Van Gelderen, John. "Asbury Revival - 1970." *Revival Focus*, 10 Mar. 2020, www.revivalfocus.org/asbury-revival-1970/.

43. Kim, Jay Y. *Analog Church: Why we need real people, places, and things in the digital age.* Intervarsity Press, 2020.

44. For a basic summary of the foundational doctrines of the Christian faith, check out *What Christians Ought to Believe* by Michael Bird (Zondervan, 2016).

45. Svigel, Michael J. *RetroChristianity: Reclaiming the Forgotten Faith.* Crossway, 2012, p. 232.

46. Garland, David E. *1 Corinthians.* Baker Academic, 2003, p. 589.

47. Todisco, Eric. "Eddie Van Halen Remembered as 'Tremendously Gifted Musician' During Rock and Roll Hall of Fame Ceremony." *Yahoo!*, Yahoo!, 2020, money.yahoo.com/eddie-van-halen-remembered-tremendously-191506961.html.

48. https://www.planobiblechapel.org/tcon/notes/html/nt/1corinthians/1corinthians.htm

49. McRae, William. *Dynamics of Spiritual Gifts.* Zondervan, 1976, p. 47.

50. Coleman, Robert. *The Master Plan of Evangelism.* Revell, 1993, p. 66.

51. Eims, Leroy. *The Lost Art of Disciple-Making.* Zondervan, 1978.

52. https://www.barna.com/research/half-churchgoers-not-heard-great-commission/

53. Cecil, Douglas M. *The 7 Principles of an Evangelistic Life.* Moody Press, 2003.